Praise for

FINDING JOY AFTER LOSS

"Here is a soulful blueprint filled with truth, beauty and vision that will lead you methodically to your authentic loving self. Just follow the author's list. If you will allow it to move through you, it will touch your heart deeply with joy where pain once existed. As a veteran widow who has known Vashon during this journey, I can honestly say it has brought me Joy seeing the light come back in her eyes."

—Carolyn Moor, Founder of Modern Widows Club
www.modernwidowsclub.com

FINDING JOY AFTER LOSS

My Seven-Step Journey of Transforming Grief into Joy

Vashon Marie Sarkisian

Published by Vashon Marie Sarkisian
Winter Park, Florida

Cover design by Audrey Phillips,
Design Studio Orlando, Inc.

Interior design & layout by The Book Couple
www.thebookcouple.com

ISBN-13: 978-0615728698

Printed in the United States of America

This book is dedicated
to my late husband,
Patrick James McCarty,
and to my son,
Kean Patrick McCarty.

I hold it true, whate'er befall;
I feel it, when I sorrow most;
'Tis better to have loved and lost
Than never to have loved at all.

—Alfred Lord Tennyson, *In Men*

Contents

Acknowledgments

This book could not have been possible without the loving support of my family and friends. Many times along the process of writing I questioned what I was doing and why I was doing this. If it had not been for the love and encouragement I received from my family and friends I would not be here with this book today.

I have to thank my friends and editors: Irene Sherlock, who first helped me with her encouraging suggestions on how to make this story come to life. My dear friend, Phyllis Corkum, who was a detective with her edits. Kim Weiss, one of my oldest and dearest friends, who also works for a well-respected book publisher. Not only did I get lots of publishing advice, but it was her loving words of encouragement during the three years of writing this book that were the most valuable to me. Carol and Gary Rosenberg, The Book Couple, who doctored this book into shape and gave me the confidence to finally share it with you.

I also want to thank my amazing, caring, and nurturing naturopathic doctor, Mandy Rae Gulla, N.D., L.M.P., who was kind enough to review and edit the section on health.

I also have to thank my late husband, Patrick, for I know on some level that along this journey he has been my biggest supporter. He helped thousands of people to heal during his lifetime, and through me he is still doing the healing.

And Kean, my son, who put up with me as I seemed to never stop writing or rewriting this book. Thank you for your patience, your unconditional love, and for being the bright light that you are. I love you.

Introduction

I started writing this journal in November 2009 as a way of processing what our family had just been through. It was days before the worst Thanksgiving of my life, a time where I was alternately numb and angry and not a bit thankful for the blow my son and I had just been dealt. Four years prior, my husband, Patrick, had been diagnosed with prostate cancer. He'd endured many visits to hospitals, lots of medication, several operations, and radiation therapy. He died on January 18, 2008. He was sixty years old.

Those first few weeks after his death, my eight-year-old son and I sleepwalked through our respective lives, coping as best we could with everyday tasks. Eventually, Kean started playing basketball and had a sleepover to celebrate his ninth birthday. I plowed through work, met friends for lunch, and considered a summer vacation. One day, I found myself smiling at my cat, Amber, who was busy chasing her tail across the lawn.

There it was . . . *boom!* . . . joy, the emotion I hadn't expected to ever feel again. Although I had been journaling for a while, I started seriously considering the process that had begun for me: this reawakening of self, albeit in fits and starts, of the person I used to be, of the person I'd become. I was forever changed, of course—different, better in some ways. But I had discovered I could feel joy again, and from that day on, I made it my mission to make that happen as frequently and as best I could.

I developed strategies and paid close attention to what did and did not work. I observed my son and wrote lots in my journal. These thoughts evolved and culminated into a plan, what has become a "joy" handbook of sorts. And this is what I present to you in this book.

The seven steps to finding joy (plus the bonus step I discovered along the way) outlined in these pages are for anyone who has been touched by devastating loss and cannot imagine that they'll ever feel anything positive again. It is for those of you who, despite your tragedy, are starting to explore the idea of engaging in life once again. It is for anyone who knows that in order to be part of life, you must do it fully and completely.

Come with me, and allow me to share my journey with you. Then, see how you, too, can find your joy.

CHAPTER 1

Our Journey

It was Thanksgiving 2007, and my husband had just eaten what would be his last real meal. We were celebrating the holiday with my parents and brother. Everyone was in high spirits, and best of all, Patrick was feeling well despite his emaciated appearance. Everything seemed almost normal that day. Does it matter that later in the day he threw up his food? I don't know. In fact, I don't claim to know anything anymore. Even sitting here at the computer, wondering what the hell I am doing writing down this story, one I want to erase from my mind and yet doesn't go away. It's the story that haunts me, prevents me from sleeping at night. The story I never dreamt would be mine—one I don't want to claim—with an ending I wish were different. A nightmare. And somehow it is mine, ours, for I have a ten-year-old son.

His perspective is different. How does he see things? What would he say—that his daddy died the day before his eighth birthday, a shadow that will forever loom in his life? "My dad died when I was very young," he might say to his therapist one day. Life and death merged into one. I could not protect my child from this pain, this injustice, this loss. Isn't it a mother's duty to protect her child? And yet, I was a victim as well.

My husband, Patrick McCarty, was diagnosed with prostate cancer in April 2005. I'll never forget that day. We heard those words in the doctor's office and all I kept thinking was *My husband is going to die.* I felt such guilt. How could I think such a thing? He would not die! This was the formidable Patrick McCarty—macrobiotic teacher and shiatsu practitioner. Patrick, who taught and counseled hundreds, if not thousands, of people to heal themselves of a wide variety of ailments, including life-threatening illnesses.

He had been macrobiotic for more than thirty years and had apprenticed under Shizuko Yamamoto, the founder of Barefoot Shiatsu, for twenty years.*

Patrick authored five books on natural health and healing that sold worldwide and were translated into eight different languages. He met with former first lady Hillary Rodham Clinton at the White House in Washington, D.C., and introduced her to information on shiatsu and preventative health care. He sponsored dozens of macrobiotic educational events

* "Macrobiotic" means *long life.* In the West, it is typically associated with a diet of whole grains, vegetables, and beans. It is believed that when eating whole foods, you can begin to create a whole life.

"Shiatsu" means *finger pressure.* It is the stimulation of the body with the hands and fingers along the meridian lines to improve the flow of qi, or energy.

throughout the United States that included featured educators such as Benjamin Spock, M.D., Dean Ornish, M.D., John McDougall, M.D., and Michio Kushi, to name a few. He traveled through the United States, Europe, and Asia lecturing and teaching workshops.

Patrick was a devoted husband and father, best friend, and lover extraordinaire. He was a brother, world traveler, public speaker, teacher, student, author, comedian, swimmer, and cook (oh, what a cook!).

What are you thinking, God? Can't you see how wrong this is?

My world crashed in all around me. Everything was caving in. I couldn't breathe. *Breathe.* I told myself to breathe. One breath at a time. Slowly, deliberately, one breath, then another. *You can do it. You've got to hold it together for your husband, your child. Keep it together, Vashon. What do I do? I have to do something. I can fix it, I can make it right! I will cook for him. I will care for him, love him, and I will bargain with God to cure him. God, please save my husband. Keep him alive. I will be so grateful when they give my husband a reprieve.*

God, tell me what to do. I'm listening.

I'm an urban planner, for God's sake. It's how I make my living. I design communities for people to live in. There is order in this. You create a master plan and the plan gets executed. It's very solid, linear, and predictable. I'm really good at it. But I wasn't good at this. This was not part of our plan. I couldn't make this right despite the fact that we had done everything right. We were good people. We lived by the rules. Didn't God make the rules? Patrick had devoted his life to helping people daily. Didn't that count for something?

Sometimes I wonder if I would have made it this far if it weren't for my child. Kean gave me the focus I needed to move through life, taking care of our necessities and at the same time helping me focus on joyful moments despite the hardships. I quickly learned to live in the moment for I could only think of our immediate needs and those things that had to be done. I would go grocery shopping. Later, I would cook dinner, and then I would spend time with Kean, reading to him from his favorite books.

Somehow I convinced myself that everything was going to be all right. And yet there was a part of me that just wanted to scream at the top of my lungs: "This is not all right! My husband has cancer and this is not all right! I am royally pissed and despondent and don't know how I'm going to keep it all together."

We tried to keep it together by living as normally as possible despite the many doctors visits and the added stress of the "C" word being used in our home. We talked about it only with family and a few close friends, who were worried sick about Patrick. Few knew the extent of his physical pain. He was having difficulty urinating, and many nights I woke up to an empty bed only to find him in the living room with acupuncture needles dotting his abdomen, legs, and hands just to help moderate the pain level.

His urologist had him on Flomax to help him urinate and Lupron to suppress testosterone in his body. Otherwise, he would die sooner than he would have from the cancer. A month after Patrick's diagnosis, he had transurethral resection of the prostate (TURP) surgery. TURP surgery is very common for men with an enlarged prostate. During surgery, a portion of the prostate was removed to allow him to urinate more freely.

We had two lives then: the brave face we put on for the public, and the other one, the private sorrowful life we mostly hid, even from ourselves because it vacillated between fear and hope.

Patrick continued to work despite the pain and fatigue. He continued to see clients at our home in Winter Park and in California, on his monthly trips. Years ago Patrick had been the director of a natural health education organization in northern California. He maintained a group of clients who depended on him for shiatsu treatments and counseling on a regular basis.

He took his time those days with clients, sometimes spending two to three hours instead of the usual one. It was as if time did not exist in the way that it used to, and this was his moment to heal, to care for his clients. He was his work, and he became the healer he always wanted to be. His clients were transformed, and they couldn't seem to get enough of him. I thought he was working too hard, pushing himself too much. But I wanted him to decide what made his life meaningful.

Our family started taking taekwondo lessons in June 2005. On some level, Patrick felt that if he could master the physical requirements of this art he could beat this thing growing inside him. A year and a half later, Kean got his black belt, and Patrick would say that he had never been more fit in his life—an irony, to be sure. We lived the illusion that everything was normal, trying to forget the awful thing growing inside my husband's body.

I met Patrick on Mother's Day in 1996. Our mutual friend, Harriet McNear, ran a macrobiotic cooking school in Winter Park, Florida, where I volunteered and taught. Patrick was in town from Eureka, California, where he had been running the East-West Center for Macrobiotics with his ex-wife for the past twenty years. He was here on business, teaching shiatsu and staying at Harriet's home.

He claimed he fell in love with me the moment he met me. He knew that he was going to marry me, he said. He loved to tell the story of how we met. That first day he walked into Harriet's kitchen, I was chopping vegetables for our evening meal. "I'm Patrick," he said with a warm smile. I had that excited, jittery feeling in my belly. *Who is this man?* I wondered. We shared a delicious meal together with Harriet and her husband, Paul. The evening was full of laughter and stories of mutual friends. Patrick felt familiar to me. The evening passed quickly, and I think we both wondered when we would we see each other again.

After his return to California, we soon began a long-distance romance with countless phone calls and as many visits as Patrick could muster to Winter Park. We married on August 8, 1998, on Vashon Island in my parents' backyard, overlooking the beautiful waters of Puget Sound.

Vashon Island is a small island just south of Seattle, Washington. My great-great-grandparents were some of the first settlers on this island. I was named after my great-grandmother, Edna O'Keefe, who was born on the island and whose middle name was Vashon. I never dreamed I would marry the love of my life there.

It was a relatively small wedding, with our closest friends and family members attending. The few days leading up to the ceremony were filled with prewedding festivities: a wedding-blessing ceremony for myself, lavish meals, preparations for the house and garden, and countless demonstrations of all of the love and support from family and friends around us as we prepared to pledge our sacred vows to each other.

Seven months later I was pregnant with our son, Kean, who was born two days before Patrick's fifty-third birthday. Life felt sweet and simple back then. My husband and I were blissfully in love, and we had a beautiful and happy child. Patrick's counseling practice was thriving, and we had just bought a modest home in Winter Park. Yes, it needed some work—a new kitchen, new bathrooms, and a lot of cosmetic changes—but we were up for the challenge.

I returned to work several months after our son was born. Because of Patrick's flexible schedule, he was able to spend a lot of time caring for Kean, making my transition back to work easier. We soon found a woman in the neighborhood, Di, who cared for children at her home. She became a second mother to Kean and their strong relationship continues to this day. Patrick was a great father, and sometimes I thought he acted more like a buddy to Kean than a parent. The two of them were always goofing around, and when not rolling around on the floor together, Patrick was giving Kean a child's introduction to Chinese medicine.

Traveling was a big part of our lives, and we were fortunate to create opportunities where Patrick could teach and we could vacation as a family. By the time Kean entered kindergarten, he had traveled to California, Mexico, France, Italy, and Japan.

Kean was five years old when Patrick was diagnosed with cancer, and the floor fell out from beneath our feet. I realized something was terribly wrong in November 2004 during our trip to Japan. Patrick was there to teach several workshops on shiatsu. He was in excruciating pain every time he tried to urinate. We both thought it was a serious urinary infection. It wasn't until April 2005 that Patrick agreed to go to a urologist. He waited until I returned home from work one day to tell me the devastating news.

"What do you mean you have cancer?" I asked.

Prostate specific antigen (PSA) were words we would hear again and again for the rest of Patrick's life. PSA is a simple blood test that measures abnormalities in the prostate. Generally, anything under a PSA of 4 is considered healthy. Anything higher than a 10 is considered abnormal. Patrick's PSA was 23. Several days later, we sat together in front of the doctor as he tried to explain Patrick's condition to us.

"You have a very large tumor on your prostate," the doctor said.

"Can't you cut it out?" I asked.

"It is too large to remove, and I would consider other forms of therapy at this stage," the doctor stated.

We drilled the doctor with questions. I took notes feverishly. We left the office feeling defeated and uncertain of the outcome.

The recommended protocol was to start Patrick on Lupron, which suppresses male hormones and was supposed to shrink the prostate tumor. By then, I was beginning to learn more about prostate cancer, previously a world totally foreign to me. Because of Patrick's occupation as a shiatsu practitioner and macrobiotic counselor, he knew quite a bit about the disease. In his work, he treated hundreds of clients who suffered from some form of cancer. Only this time, he was the patient—something he never imagined would happen. He was devastated and felt defeated.

Alone with my own thoughts, I couldn't help but be angry with my husband. *Why hadn't Patrick seen a doctor sooner? Could this whole situation have been averted had he paid attention to the signs? There had to have been signs. He had to have known something was wrong, so why didn't he do something about it sooner?*

I felt intense anger at times wondering why he had gambled his life. Our lives! Yet, as angry as I felt, I knew I had to move beyond these feelings and support him unconditionally in his recovery.

How does someone who's been in the holistic health profession for more than thirty years go about treating his own cancer? How would my husband find the balance between Western medicine and his familiar Eastern holistic approach? Not surprisingly, Patrick opted to mix the two.

Here are some of the things he tried:

1. A cleaner macrobiotic diet. Generally, Patrick rarely veered from eating macrobiotically, but things were more strict now. His diet became bland and pure, nothing but brown rice, steamed vegetables, miso soup, pickles, and sea veggies.
2. Fasting for a week at a time.
3. Supplements including Chinese herbs, megadoses of vitamin C, prostate support supplements, and a host of other things, which, for the life of me, I cannot remember.
4. Daily servings of magosteen juice and goji juice.
5. Meditation three times a day for up to several hours at a time.
6. Daily use of the RIFE machine. This device emits a frequency of light that is claimed to destroy cancer cells.
7. A lighter client load. But, as I said before, he spent more time with each patient and seemed to take more pleasure from the whole process.
8. Travels to China, India, Japan, and South America. Patrick was on a spiritual quest, and I think he found much of what he was looking for in the temples of China, the mountains of Mount Abu, the gardens of Japan, and the village of Abadiania.
9. Study. He learned additional healing modalities, which he was able to incorporate into his practice. He added Heartmath, Pranic Healing, and emotional freedom techniques (EFT), to name a few.

10. Exercise: swimming, taekwondo, and chi gong.
11. Heart-to-heart communication with family, friends, and clients.
12. Clearing unresolved issues with family and friends.

In spite of all these positive activities, a fear set in, due in part to our interactions with the medical community. We received a second opinion from a doctor at MD Anderson, who delivered the news that Patrick had a rising PSA. This prognosis meant that he had five years at best, and only if he considered immediate or even experimental treatment. Patrick decided to start radiation therapy. As I said, we'd been told the tumor was too big to remove, so surgery was not an option.

Patrick had tried since April to treat his cancer naturally to no avail. He felt he had no other choice but to begin the first of forty-nine treatments in November 2005. These treatments would last three months, with trips to the hospital twice a week. Patrick responded well to the radiation treatments, with little or no side effects. His PSA dropped to 2.5 by February 2006. He was hopeful. I was ecstatic.

Why hadn't the macrobiotic diet worked for Patrick, or had it?

Before his birth, Patrick's mother had taken diethylstilbestrol (DES), a drug that was supposed to prevent miscarriages. Research later revealed that children born to women who had taken DES were much more prone to develop ovarian or prostate cancer. Was this why Patrick developed prostate cancer? Had he not been macrobiotic would his life have been even shorter? We will never know.

Prior to my husband's diagnosis, I had never thought much about death. Why would I? We were both fairly young and had always been healthy. Death was the last thing on our minds. We were macrobiotic after all. Didn't that count for something? We ate organically; we were discriminating about the types and quality of products we bought; we recycled our paper and bottles; we meditated and did yoga. We had a simple life and were raising our child to make healthy choices. We did everything "right," so how could death come knocking on our door? After Patrick's diagnosis, I thought about death all the time.

Mary Morgan, a good friend of my husband's, was married to the well-known Dr. Spock. When the good doctor passed away, Mary threw a raucous party in her husband's honor. My mother wondered aloud, "How could she celebrate at her own husband's funeral?" I remember thinking, *Wow, this lady may know something I don't know.*

I had the privilege of speaking with her afterward, and yes, she was mourning Ben's passing, but she talked about how he had had a long and fruitful life. She wanted to commemorate and remember the beautiful times they shared. Patrick was fifty-eight when he was diagnosed. Our circumstances were different, but could I learn from Mary?

All around me I saw nothing but couples, particularly elderly couples. We were in Florida, after all, where lots of elderly couples come to retire. But I was wondering if Patrick and I would grow old together? Would we see our child grow up, marry, and have his own children? Would we be grandparents together? Would Patrick live to celebrate Kean's future birthdays? Would he help Kean with his homework, see him perform in school plays and compete in sporting events? Would he advise his son about girls, offer driving lessons, take him fishing and hiking and canoeing and swimming? Would they watch football together, cheer for their favorite team while drinking beer? Would Patrick live to teach Kean acupuncture, shiatsu, and Chinese medicine? Would Kean grow up with his father or without him? What was going to happen to my little Kean? What would happen to me?

In August 2006, six months after Patrick had finished his radiation treatments, he was scheduled for his follow up PSA test. This test would let the doctors know how effective the radiation treatment had been and if he was in remission. The signs were not good. His PSA had jumped to 25.5.

What happened? How could this be? It must be a mistake.

"Do the test over!" I begged.

A week later, his PSA had risen to 37.5. We were devastated. The solution was to start Patrick on Lupron injections again. His PSA went down to 1.5 in October. We became hopeful once again.

That same month, Patrick traveled to Mount Abu, India, and spent two weeks meditating at an ashram. He loved this country and its people, and he couldn't wait to return with his family so he could share the richness of this country with us. "You would love it," he said.

In January of 2007, Patrick turned sixty years old. One

way or another, I was determined to make that year one of celebration. We started off the year with a two-week vacation in Kyoto, Japan. Patrick loved Japan. This was his eighth trip, my third, and Kean's second. Patrick moved gracefully through the country. Nothing seemed to faze him. He could read Japanese and maneuver through the train system. He knew what to order at restaurants and how to converse with strangers. He knew the villages he wanted to visit, the temples that sang to his heart, the gardens that inspired him. Patrick was at home there. The cherry blossoms were just beginning to bloom and the gardens were alive with color and beauty. The hot baths soothed his body, the temples his soul. We drank green tea like Americans drink water. We were alive and felt nourished.

2007 started off being a good year. We were hopeful and optimistic, though I did wonder what we would do if the cancer came back. *Could he beat it again? Could we survive as a family?* I'm sure a day did not go by without each of us having our private thoughts, wondering, fearing, and praying that everything was going to be all right.

In April 2007, Patrick's PSA jumped to 11.7. *What do we do now? Is there anything we can do to make this thing go away?*

May 2007: PSA—15.4

In May, Patrick was off to visit "John of God," a spiritual healer and psychic surgeon who lived in a remote village in Abadiania, Brazil. Thousands of people traveled annually to visit him, hoping for a miracle, hoping for the answer that would give them back their lives.

Is Patrick going to be healed? I wondered.

On some level I'm sure he was healed, if not physically, certainly spiritually. He was calmer, more sure of himself.

In that past year and a half, Patrick had traveled to China, Japan, India, and Brazil, and monthly to California. The amount of traveling seemed ludicrous. How taxing it must have been on his body, and it was creating a financial burden on our family. But how could I deny my husband the opportunity to discover what he needed to heal himself? You can't put a price on finding a cure for the person you love.

June 2007: PSA—39.5

In July we made our annual trip to California to visit with family and friends and to attend the French Meadows Summer Camp in Tahoe National Forest. This very primitive outdoor camp is where the nation's top macrobiotic teachers gather to teach. For more than twenty years, French Meadows had been Patrick's pilgrimage, and it had become ours. We looked forward to seeing family and old friends each year, and it was our chance to connect with one another. We considered this our time to slow down, to revisit our dreams as a couple and family, and commune with nature. But this year was different. Patrick was going to make public the news that he had advanced prostate cancer. It would be a confession of sorts, admitting to friends and peers that he, Patrick McCarty, had cancer. He was not invincible. He was human, after all.

That year he was the morning's featured speaker. How would he dazzle them? *What did he have up his sleeve?* people wondered. My husband was a popular man—articulate, charismatic, and an entertaining and engaging speaker. Patrick was constantly learning new things about the health field and incorporating them into his teachings and his practice. Little did they know he was ready to bare his soul, to share with this group of loving and nurturing friends—people who adored him—that he was suffering from cancer.

He worried that those new to the world of macrobiotics would be discouraged about the authenticity of the field. How was it possible that a respected teacher and practitioner, who followed every rule of the profession, could succumb to cancer? Macrobiotics was an alternative discipline that many people followed when faced with life-threatening diseases. If Patrick had cancer, then anybody could get cancer. Nobody was safe.

After finishing breakfast, I took Kean to kids camp while Patrick prepared for his morning talk. He seemed nervous, fidgety, and unsure of himself.

"Are you all right?" I asked, knowing he was not.

"I don't know how I will tell them the news," he said.

I held him close to me, knowing that no words could soothe him and hoping that my presence could ease his heart, if only a bit.

The lecture area was outdoors under the canopy of stately ponderosa pines. Patrick stood in front of the chalkboard as people gathered around with folding chairs and notepads. Patrick had such a good sense of humor, and he opened the talk with a few jokes. After he had everyone's attention, he dove right in.

"I have news that may be very disturbing for some of you and shocking to others," he said.

The moment was such a contrast to the beautiful day: the morning sun shining through the trees, the smell of pine needles, the birds chirping, and the faint buzz of early morning insects. Being at this place was life at its best, yet there stood my husband, ready to talk about death. He went on and told them his story and how he was melding Eastern and Western medicine to find a cure. He was optimistic, and he gave them hope that he would survive and that his cancer could be beaten. And I sat there and listened. My heart ached for him and for the uncertainty of what was ahead.

I don't remember much else about camp that year. I remember the pain Patrick was experiencing again each time he had to urinate. I remember he worked long and hard hours with his clients. I remember the love and support we felt from everyone at camp. And I'll never forget the talent show that last night where Patrick and Kean performed taekwondo moves for an appreciative audience. The two of them took a bow, sweating and smiling at the crowd. They clearly were the winners of this talent show. Despite his illness, my husband still had the ability to lose himself in the pleasure of the moment. He could still entertain, and this made him happy.

September: PSA—273

Patrick was in Atlanta for the weekend at a workshop on EFT or Tapping. He called to say that after his morning swim his whole body was aching. At first feeling it was the swim, he soon realized this unfamiliar feeling was something in his body that was more than just aches and pains. He was feeling so bad that he wasn't sure he could finish the workshop.

"I just want to come home," he said from his hotel room.

"Honey, come home," I said.

Patrick was scheduled for a follow up CT and bone scan. A week later, we received the results. His PSA had jumped to 273 and the scans showed his cancer had spread to his skull, neck, ribs, spine, and pelvic area. Patrick had less than a year to live, the doctor said. Neither one of us spoke. The doctor cleared his throat.

"I advise you to get your affairs in order," he said.

Patrick was sure this meant that he was at the end of his life. I spent the next day in bed under the covers, barely able to move. What would I do without my husband, my love, my rock?

The following day while our son was at school, the two of us sat at the kitchen table, making a plan. It was time for drastic measures. Patrick would start looking into alternative clinics that dealt with life-threatening illnesses.

On September 10, Patrick gave his last shiatsu treatment in Orlando to an elderly woman he had been treating for the past several years. The following week, he flew to California to tell his clients that he would not be able to return to California for a while. He was doing poorly and would be taking some time off. It was the most difficult trip he had ever made, he told me when he got back. These people were his friends, his family. He was their teacher and healer. Many asked what they would do without him.

Patrick had a client, Kevin, who he had been treating in California for more than twenty years. Kevin financially made Patrick's trips to the west coast very attractive. Patrick had helped Kevin overcome many health issues with which the medical community had little success. On this trip, he spoke with Kevin about the possibility of loaning him money for treatment at an alternative clinic. Kevin assured Patrick he would pay for all of our out-of-pocket medical bills, including Kean's education if anything should happen to Patrick. This pledge was beyond anything we could have hoped for. To know we could pursue treatment and not worry about the financial burden was truly a gift.

We flew to Houston the following month for treatment at an alternative cancer clinic. The clinic specialized in an experimental therapy called antineoplaston therapy, which was claimed to kill off cancer cells. Unfortunately, Patrick reacted horribly to the medication, losing twenty pounds in several weeks. We decided it was time to find a different place for his care.

Three weeks later we were off to Mexico to check Patrick into a progressive residential clinic that specialized in the treatment of cancer. In addition to Western medicine, they incorporated Eastern holistic therapies to determine the best approach to health care for each individual. We were in survival mode.

Patrick spent three and a half weeks there being treated with everything from psychological counseling to various forms of physical therapies and a wide variety of medicines, ranging from natural supplements to very strong pain medications. I was able take off time from work to spend the first week with him, and then I returned the last week to bring him home. Kean stayed at my parents' house in between my various trips. Patrick's dear and long-time friend Steve Miller looked after him while I was back in Orlando caring for Kean.

The medical team put Patrick through a very comprehensive and thorough analysis to determine his current condition. After this evaluation, a treatment plan, which varied daily, was devised to help Patrick fight the tumor. A typical day started with a host of supplements, lemon water to detox the liver, followed by a shot of wheat grass, and then twenty minutes with the RIFE machine. Just before breakfast he would meet with the doctor assigned to him to review records and protocol and discuss how his treatment was going. After breakfast he met with the clinic's psychologist and then he was off to receive intravenous therapy to help detoxify his body of heavy metals. The afternoons were spent in ultraviolet therapy to stimulate the immune system, colonics, homeopathy, and lymphatic drainage massage, to name a few practices. Pain medication, specific cancer-related drugs, and supplements were given throughout the day. Protocol would vary depending on the recommendations of his doctors in the mornings.

By the time I returned to Mexico to collect my husband, Patrick had lost much more weight; he was pale and his skin had a yellowish hue. The stories I heard of his time at the clinic while I was away were not pretty. Patrick was sleeping all the time. He could barely tolerate the treatments assigned specifically for him. He was hardly eating at all. *How was he still holding on? How would I get him home in this condition? What were we going to do now?*

On one of our afternoons in Mexico, a man came up to me as I was swimming in the pool and told me about his wife who had died of cancer several years earlier. He had written a book about their experience and wanted to know if I would be interested in reading it. I looked at him, considering his kind eyes.

I was enraged. *Why is he telling me this?* I wondered. *What does his book on death have to do with me? I am not going to lose my husband. I do not want to understand what they'd gone through. That's his story, not mine.*

"No, I do not want to read the book," I told him, and I swam off to do more laps.

Despite the doctor's prognosis and Patrick's emaciated, weakened appearance, I still believed he was going to beat this disease. Somehow he would. Didn't everyone else know this, too?

The clinic recommended a procedure called "specific transfer factor." It was a surgical procedure performed at the clinic, where they would remove a small portion of Patrick's hip bone to create a special vaccine for him. We would have to wait six weeks for the vaccine to finally arrive in Orlando.

The closing comments on Patrick's release chart read: "Patrick J. McCarty has enough intrinsic dynamic to turn disease processes into healing ones."

We left the clinic reluctantly yet feeling hopeful that the vaccine would be his ticket back to life. We also left with a huge bill that was charged to Patrick's credit card. While in Mexico, Patrick had called Kevin several times to let him know how he was doing and to update him about our mounting medical bills. We hoped we could still depend on his word.

Our trip home was long and painful. Patrick was terribly sick on the plane. I wondered how I would be able to care for him upon our return. *What lay ahead of us? Could we do this on our own? Should Patrick have stayed in Mexico?* We waited for the vaccine to arrive, hoping it was going to save him, hoping for a cure.

In the days following our return, Patrick deteriorated quickly. This once 165-pound man barely weighed 120 pounds. I worried about Kean, who was only seven years old. What would he think when he saw his father like this? What did his young eyes see? Was he able to process what was happening around him? His father was no longer the father he knew, but this stranger with a body that was failing him. How could I protect my child from this horror? All I could do was hold him and tell him his father was very sick and that we were hoping his daddy would get better soon.

"When?" Kean asked.

I looked at him tenderly as tears welled up in my eyes. "I don't know, honey," I answered.

Did he believe me? Did he know the truth? Was I wrong to give him hope? Did he wonder why his father couldn't play with him anymore? Did he understand the severity of his father's illness?

November 2007: PSA—1,286

"How high can one's PSA go?" I asked the doctor.

Patrick was by now confined to the house. He moved from the bedroom to the couch and back to the bedroom again.

This was his world now. He stared through our French doors at the lake and beyond. He loved this view where he could watch the ducks fly by and contemplate the stillness of the water. He had always loved our home. He said he knew it was ours the moment he saw it. I believe the small lake in our backyard represented for him the ocean he longed for, the ever-healing ocean he so loved.

We decided that it was time to reach out to our loving community of family and friends. We had been stoically carrying the weight of this illness on just a few shoulders. We needed to share our journey and welcome our friends into this time in our lives.

Below is a copy of the letter that my dear friend Kim Weiss sent out to many of the wonderful people we knew. It was time to ask for help, but were we too late? Should we have asked sooner? Would God hear our cries at this late stage?

Dear Friends, Colleagues, and Extended Family,

This letter is coming from Kim Weiss, longtime friend of Vashon and Patrick and writing to you on their behalf. . . .

As some of you already know, three years ago, Patrick was diagnosed with advanced prostate cancer. Since then he has been fighting hard to win the battle against this awful disease. He has undergone a variety of treatments to do so and most recently returned from Mexico where he received one the most revolutionary holistic protocols to date. It's been an exhausting road for them.

Needless to say, life has turned upside down for both Patrick and Vashon, and they've been holding up amazingly well in the process. However, Patrick's condition is quite fragile and he's exercising his amazing ability to stay positive and hopeful. Hearing his voice, one finds it hard to believe he is physically challenged.

As their good friend, Patrick and Vashon asked me to reach out to you so you can put Patrick in your heart and especially in your prayers. They sincerely believe in the power of positive energy and healing and know there's power in numbers.

So, on behalf of them, please do what you can to send loving thoughts and healing prayers to Patrick, and to Vashon, and Kean. It would mean so much to them.

They send you their love,

Kim

Our good friend and physician, Ricky, suggested that I call hospice. He said it was too much for me to monitor Patrick's medication, and his pain level was way out of control.

My mind screamed, *Hospice! Isn't that for people who are at the end stage of their life? Does Ricky think Patrick is dying?*

Ricky assured me that hospice were the experts in administering medication and that they would be of great assistance to me. Two weeks later I called hospice and signed a paper stating that Patrick had less than six months to live. *The absurdity of it all! My husband is not going to die!*

I told myself it was just a means to an end, that I needed help and they were the pain-management experts. We were assigned a fabulous nurse, Amy, who stopped by the house twice a week to monitor Patrick's morphine levels, which were increasing as the weeks passed.

I had gone back to work after our return from Mexico. My parents lived just down the street and my father visited Patrick daily, for hours on end, keeping him company and helping him in any way that he could. Several people from the office volunteered to visit during their lunch breaks. They visited with and read to him. I felt that he was in good hands during the day, which allowed me to focus as best as I could at the office.

Amy's weekly visits to our house soon turned into daily visits. We soon acquired a walker and a hospital bed. Patrick deteriorated so quickly that it was hard to imagine he was the same man as just a few months before.

Though his body was failing him, the essence of my husband continued to shine through. He had so much grace and beauty during this horrendously challenging time. Never did he complain or express regret about anything other than his fear of leaving me and Kean alone.

"Vashon, I am really okay with dying," he said one afternoon when we were alone. I started to cry. "I just can't stand the thought of leaving you and Kean."

As usual, he was thinking about our loss more than his own. And through all of this, he managed to find joy in the smallest details of life. A song on the stereo. Ducks circling our lake. A moment with his son before bed. A comforting word from a friend. Afternoon visits from my father.

He became my teacher once again, modeling strength and determination so I could face the awfulness of what lay ahead.

December 2007: PSA—1,286

December, the month that is supposed to be filled with poinsettias, gingerbread cookies, and carolers. The month of family and friends. Did Kean have his photo taken with Santa that year? I don't remember much of that month, just that our son's innocent childhood energy was a bit much for Patrick. I tried to find a sense of balance that would work for both of them. I tried to give them both what they needed. Mother, spouse, nurse, breadwinner, and confessor.

Our friends Steve and Yvonne visited from California. It was great for Patrick to spend time with his dear friends. Sometimes he had quiet days. On other days there were long conversations among us all. By this time, Patrick figured out that smoking marijuana helped with pain management. We were prepared to do anything for his comfort. Patrick's PSA had gone up another 266 points and was hovering at 1,552.

It hardly seemed possible that he was still functioning. The subject didn't come up. What did it matter? The facts were that my husband had withered away to almost nothing. He barely ate, and simply moving was an effort. The walker was his constant companion. Despite it all, we managed to celebrate New Year's Eve with Steve and Yvonne. We raised our glasses and toasted each other.

"I love you, Vashon," Patrick whispered. Then he kissed me as if it were any other year.

"I love you, sweetie," I said.

January 2008

I used to pray that Patrick would be healed. By this time, I prayed that he would not have to suffer much more. He was in so much pain that we had to double and then triple his pain medication. I feared that I would have Patrick in body only. I hoped he could adjust to the medication and yet still find some lucid moments of joy, conversation, reflection, and love. I watched him sleep and feared there was little left in him. Though he'd been ill for three years now, the ending seemed to be coming fast. How much longer could he hold on?

We were getting a lot of support from family, friends, and colleagues. A Zen garden was being installed in the side yard, next to the picture window in our living room. Colleagues were building a tree house for Kean. Friends were cooking meals, taking turns reading to Patrick, and visiting on a regular basis. I was grateful for this 24/7 care. Despite the support, the distress and ever-present sadness were excruciating at times. Kean seemed to be managing somehow, but I knew he would pay an eventual price. I had started looking for a therapist to help answer his many questions about his father's cancer and to eventually help him cope with his loss.

"Is Daddy going to die?" Kean asked.

"I think so, honey," I answered him as I held him tight.

We put the hospital bed in the family room because we didn't have any room for it anywhere else. I told myself that it was much more comfortable for Patrick to sleep in this bed than the one we used to share. He could adjust the head and feet with the press of a button. Kean loved playing with all the buttons.

"Look, Kean, we've got a bed in the family room. Isn't that silly?" said Patrick. Even I laughed at this.

At one in the morning on January 13, I woke up to Patrick's desperate calls. He'd been throwing up dark brown stuff and could no longer move his legs. He was stricken. I had never seen him this scared, and I tried to say a few words to make him feel better. But I was frightened. The hospice nurse on call said it sounded like spinal-cord compression and that I need to call 911 and get him transferred to the hospital immediately.

My parents came over as quickly as they could, and my mother took Kean home with her. A few minutes later, fire and rescue trucks were parked on the street in front of our house. I watched helplessly as six large men in all their gear rolled my husband out to the street. My father and I followed the ambulance to the hospital. Patrick was placed in the emergency ward and made as comfortable as possible until he was transferred to a room on the cancer ward. We waited for what seemed to be an eternity for information on what was really happening to my husband.

The doctor finally came and suggested a CAT scan and additional tests to determine what was happening to Patrick's body. Patrick, though semicoherent, was clear that he did not want additional tests and would not endure another CAT scan. I was numb and could not think straight. After the doctor left, the nurse assigned to us pulled me aside and asked what I would do with the test results. Was I going to treat him?

I stared hard at her. *What is she asking me?* I wondered, trying to process the question.

"No," I finally said and thanked her.

Patrick was transferred to the cancer ward. There, in his room with bags and bottles and IVs and machines attached to him, I sat next to him and monitored his life. He was in and out of consciousness now, and he looked defeated.

Hadn't he just lost mobility in his legs? Wasn't this the next hurdle? When can we get him home?

Sunday dragged on. I left for the evening to care for Kean and to get some sleep.

Monday morning at 8:00, the oncologist called me to say that Patrick was in miserable condition and had less than three days to live.

What is he saying to me? I wondered. *This can't be right. There must be some sort of mistake.*

I told him that I would be right there, to please wait for me, that I needed to talk to him in person.

"I can't wait. I have rounds to make," the doctor said casually.

I was too upset to care, yet I wondered what kind of doctor could act so callously. Then I realized it was the kind who saw death every day.

Fortunately, my mother had taken Kean to school that morning, so I raced to the hospital, feeling guilty that I slept in my bed the night before. I could have been there to comfort my husband, who needed me.

I called Amy, our hospice nurse, who arrived at noon and worked with the hospital to get Patrick released and to get him home. They wanted to keep him at the hospital to run more tests. I wanted my husband to die at home. It's what he wanted, too.

While we waited for Patrick's transfer home, I helped him make several phones calls: to his brother Mike, to his teacher Shizuko Yamamoto, and to Steve Miller, his best friend. He was eloquent as he talked to each of them, expressing his love and saying his good-byes, and he was emotionally spent when he was done. I marveled at his composure and his clarity, knowing that it was his time. Again, his only regret was leaving us. He was ready. He was in so much pain, his body no longer his. He wanted to go home.

When we finally returned to our house late Monday evening, it felt like an eternity had passed since we'd left. *How could so much happen in thirty-six hours?* I wondered. *What will the next thirty-six be like?* Hospice arrived shortly after our return home. They would be with us until the very end. We tried to make Patrick as comfortable as possible. He was so relieved to be in the safety of our home.

My parents wondered if they should keep Kean at their house. I knew that Kean needed to be home and be part of his father's transition. I had decided that Kean would stay home from school as well. I told Kean that we now knew that his daddy was dying and that he would only be with us a few more days. Tears welled up in his eyes as I told him the inevitable facts. I held him tightly as we both cried and as the flow of tears never seemed to end.

Kean was by this time sleeping in my bed. What did he think? We did not plan this for our child. We had so many dreams together. What happened to them all?

Patrick was in and out of consciousness. It was so late. The nurse suggested that I go to bed. I didn't want to leave him so I made a bed on the couch. I had to be next to him in case he was ready to leave. She suggested that I say my good-byes and she left the room. How would we say good-bye?

Patrick was lying there massaging my hand, giving me a shiatsu treatment. He was telling me to breathe in and breathe out, breathe in and breathe out, breathe in and breathe out. . . . Forever the teacher, forever the healer. Thinking of me, even in his last moments.

I told him how much I loved him, that I would always miss him and that it was okay for him to leave us.

"I love you, Vashon, and I want you to love again," he whispered.

I just sat with him, holding him, telling him it was all going to be okay. And on some level, somewhere beyond the sorrow, I could feel that it would be.

Patrick made it through the night. We rolled his bed into the living room, facing the newly installed Zen garden. This room was more peaceful. We had candles burning throughout the room and soft devotional music playing. Sacred text and scripture was being read to him throughout the day. Talking was reserved for another room. This was Patrick's space. It was time to hold Patrick in this peaceful, loving, and sacred space.

He lost consciousness, but his body was holding on. The nurses were amazed at how tranquil he was. This was usually not the case, they said, and most often there is so much suffering all the way to the end.

My friends Krista and Janice had been at the house since Tuesday, looking after Kean and monitoring activities so I could focus on Patrick. My sister Fawn and my friend Kim arrived on Thursday and gave Krista and Janice a break.

My sisters, my anchors, my friends. I could not have done it without them. I was humbled by their devotion and their love.

Thursday, 4:00 p.m., I started crying uncontrollably. Patrick's body was still with us, but he was gone. I put pictures of his deceased mother and father next to him so they would be there to help him make his transition smoother. I wanted them to be there to greet him and welcome him home.

Kean's birthday was Saturday, January 19. He would turn eight years old. My good friend Di had offered to take him and his friends for an early birthday celebration: bowling and then for a sleepover at her house. She was my angel. I told Kean to say good-bye to daddy in case he died while he was away. Kean walked over to the bed, and touching his father's hand, whispered, "Bye. I love you, Daddy." I fought back the tears as I pushed Kean out the door to celebrate his birthday.

"Have fun!" I yelled.

I did not want Patrick to die on Kean's birthday. I leaned over Patrick's bed and begged him not to die on Kean's day. Could he hear me? I had been talking to him all week, but this would be my last request. I told him he could not leave us on Kean's special day.

And on January 18, 2008, at 5:30 p.m., my dear husband, Patrick, died in our home, surrounded by his family and friends.

This is not the right story; it is all wrong. How do I capture that week? How do I do justice to Patrick? By writing this all down, do I minimize his life and subsequent death? How do I convey to my son that amidst the sorrow, amidst the pain, amidst the suffering, there *was* beauty?

Take me out of the picture. Take Kean out, and what do you have? You have a man who was between two worlds, a man whose body was dying and yet a man who was going home. He was going home to God, to his family and friends, to the next phase of his life. He was going home and would no longer suffer.

Somewhere in all the chaos there was the sweetness of being able to hold that space for Patrick. The beauty of energetically holding my husband so that he could pass in the space of love. Holding him like a mother holds her baby. Total holding, total trust, and letting go to safely move on.

Those few moments of feeling connected to God quickly eroded when reality set in. I watched as the undertaker wheeled my husband's body out the door and then placed him in the waiting black hearse. It's an image that will forever be ingrained in my mind. Later that night, my sister asked me if I would like her to sleep with me in my bed. It was the most nurturing thing she could have done for me.

Patrick's memorial service was held at Mead Gardens, which was Kean's and his father's favorite place to visit. They spent many afternoons visiting this natural park filled with wetlands, wildflowers, and wildlife. Family, friends, clients, and colleagues filled the rustic arena where the simple and elegant eulogy was performed. Kean ran around with his classmates, playing tag and picking flowers. The last time my father had escorted me was at my wedding ceremony. This time it was to honor Patrick's life. I sat and watched in disbelief, wondering how all this was happening yet feeling blessed that so many people had traveled so far to honor my husband.

The days passed and I was in a fog, going through the motions but not really present. Where was I in all of this? I searched my journal. It was hard to read, hard to tap into the darkness and despair that overwhelmed me. It was hard to remember. Disbelief, shock, and great sorrow composed the theme of my life.

I listened to the song "Not As We," and it felt as if Alanis Morisette wrote it just for me: "Day one, day one, start over again. Step one, step one, I'm barely making sense; just yet I'm faking it till I'm pseudo making it. From scratch, begin again, but this time I as 'I' and not as 'we.'"

It felt like I was faking it, and I was to a certain extent. I went to work and, on some level, work was soothing because it kept me busy. I had moments where I didn't have to think about anything else but my job. On the other hand, it was all so hypocritical. *How could I go back to work after I had watched my husband suffer and die? How could I pretend that it is all okay and that life simply goes on?* And yet I did, for I had no other choice. I had to remind myself that there is some kind of normalcy in this world and I somehow needed to be part of it. Somehow I had to survive this tragic reality for myself, but even more so for my son.

Throughout it all, Kean was my anchor. He kept me going. Somehow he kept me on this earth. I had to get through this for him. I had to find some sense of normalcy in life after the tragedy of death. *Where was Kean in all of it? Did he really comprehend what had just happened to his father?* On some level, I think he understood more than I did. He didn't have all the conditioning I had. He was innocent and he was living in the now. Sure he missed his father. Sure he was terribly sad and confused, but on some level, he was also able to live in the moment. *Could I learn from him? Could I follow in the footsteps of a child, my child?*

I remember a day when the three of us were driving to Home Depot to buy plants for the garden. We were expanding one of the planting beds and wanted to add more color to that area of the garden. I suddenly burst into tears with the knowledge that on some higher level Patrick's cancer was here to help transform all of our lives. Patrick was sacrificing his life so that we could live our lives more fully. We discussed this idea in length, knowing its truth, and at the time, not fully realizing what the outcome would be. I reflected on that first year and still wondered how this experience, this loss, could transform us.

I saw symbols of Patrick everywhere. He was in the butterflies dancing in the backyard. He was in the drugstore as they played our wedding song, "I Say a Little Prayer for You." I saw him on my son's face, in the movements he made and in the sound of his voice. He was the breeze that blew through my hair as I walked outdoors and the tickle on my ear as I was falling asleep. He was the bells ringing in the living room, telling me it was time to get up. And he was the man who haunted me in my dreams at night, forever leaving me. Gone.

Patrick was gone, and yet I felt his presence everywhere in the house, not as a single energy but one that filtered through the rooms and felt beyond time and space. It was the most amazing sensation for I had never before felt him in this way. Yet when I allowed myself to feel him, he was unlimited and expansive. In a strange way, it felt very nurturing. Patrick's energy was in the house for months after he died. I think that is why I took so much comfort from being at home. Somehow Patrick was still there. Leaving the house meant I was leaving him, and it made me feel empty and alone. The world outside felt unsafe.

There were other small incidents that made me feel Patrick's presence, but I have to say I was also very angry with him. I wanted him alive. I didn't want him in the form of the wind blowing my hair. I wanted Patrick himself moving my hair. *Where was Patrick and why did he have to die?* I could not make sense of it and that was one of the most disturbing sensations. There was no good reason for any of this. It seemed so indiscriminate. If Patrick could die, then anything could happen in life. No one was safe.

Yes, I understand it was probably the DES that killed Patrick. That was the hard fact. But there was still something unsettling to me, still something that was not right about anything that had happened.

I read every book I could get my hands on about the afterlife. *What was Patrick doing? Where had he gone? Was he happy?*

Could he see us? Was he trying to communicate with us? Could I communicate with him? Did I want to? If I was able to contact him, would it mean he was really dead? I was not ready to go there.

Six months after Patrick's death, I felt it was time to start going through his belongings. My excuse was that there were bugs in the kitchen cupboards. Patrick kept medicinal Chinese herbs and macrobiotic food in the cupboards and throughout the refrigerator. He was forever concocting a remedy for clients, family members, or himself. I am sure he was a chemist in a past life. He would make a pudding out of dried roots, add some agave syrup and kuzu (a powder made from kuzu root and used as a thickening agent in desserts, sauces, and gravies), and call it dessert. And we were his guinea pigs, whether we liked it or not!

To clean out the closet and pack up some of his things for Goodwill felt like a tremendous disloyalty. Throwing out his Chinese herbs, medicines he used to heal people, made me feel as if I was throwing away an important part of him. And yet I did it. Bit by bit, I managed to pack up what had been Patrick: the memories, mementos, relics that represented his life. Some I stored. Others I put aside until I could figure out what to do with them. I kept many of his books and papers, but I began to have no problem throwing away every jar of smelly herb he left behind in the cupboard.

I had to decide what Kean would want later to help him remember his father. I had to pack away a few precious items in a box for my son to explore at a later date. He was eight years old. He would want these things of his father's one day.

How was it possible that a person's life could be reduced to a few mere boxes?

We started a memory journal that included every memory of his father that Kean could recall.

"I remember when . . . ." he'd write, much of it misspelled.

> I like going to summer cap wiht Dad. Swimming wiht Dad. Hicking with Dad, slipping in the tent wiht Dad, going to the camp fire,
>
> I like driving to karate with daddy and mommy. Exercising with daddy. Fighting with daddy.
>
> I like going in the big budda with daddy. The hot baths. Eating sushi, going on the train, sleeping on the floor, going to the fish market, going to the gardens, going to the temples, eating mochi, seeing snow, drenging tea, eating on the floor, waering kimonos, pokemon store, takinf off our stoes, the hor springs, the tea farm the deparment stores.
>
> I like to canow whith daddy.
>
> I loke going to Mead grandens. show daddy the paths, show daddy the eggs, whake aownd the ducl lack.
>
> Daddy youst to say to mey thet the water jets are monsters under grown and when thay sneeze bubbles come up fur the day.
>
> I liked it when daddy would build sandcastles at the beach with me.

A memory journal. It sounded so absurd. Will he really remember or will his memory statements become memories themselves? Who was going to build sandcastles with Kean now? And would memories of his father simply wash away, consumed by the ocean?

Where is my memory journal? I wondered. I started keeping one, too, that later became the bones of this book. *Was I getting beyond his illness and death so I could tap into the memories of life and joy?*

The day Patrick was diagnosed was the day I let go of everything. Before this, I had been the "planner" who kept a list of things to do, to accomplish. But this habit quickly faded after Patrick's diagnosis. My to-do list was replaced with uncertainty, or maybe it had always been there, but I hadn't seen it. The truth is, planning is all an illusion. We often don't know what *to do* next.

After Patrick got sick, we changed our ways. It no longer mattered whether we packed our weekends with activities. We used our time to relax and be together. Weekends were spent going to the beach, taking long walks at Mead Gardens, hanging out at the house, playing with Kean, swimming at the YMCA, eating popcorn and watching movies on TV. We visited friends and family and took short road trips. Life became very simple in many ways. We slowed down and started to live in the now. Why did it take a life-threatening illness for us to do this?

In some ways, I had never lived more fully than I did after Patrick's diagnosis. I quickly saw that if I thought about the future then I would be in fear, afraid of what might happen. Every possible scenario would surge through my brain. When I thought about the past, I became angry. *Why didn't we do it this way? Should we have done this treatment or that? If only we had caught it sooner.*

The only joy was to be in the moment. It was the only

place I had control of my life. It was the only place where I could be available to Patrick and to Kean and to myself. I will not say that I was not fearful or angry, but I found myself more and more living in the present. As Patrick's condition worsened, it was the only place I could be. I had to pay attention and respond to our immediate needs.

I still have moments and days of anger. I blame God for this hardship imposed on our family, for the pain that Patrick had endured and that my son would grow up without a father. *How could this happen to OUR family?* I was mystified by the injustice of it all. None of it made sense to me. I remember having the illusion that life should move in a particular way. If you did A and you did B, then you would get C. But I discovered there was no surety about anything in life. We did A and B and we got S and M and F, and nothing made sense. It was all out of order, and I didn't understand life anymore. And what the f*** did it all mean?

Before Patrick's diagnosis, I felt like I was walking on solid ground. It didn't matter whether it was true or not. It was my perception. My reality now is that there is nothing solid under my feet anymore. I could fall and just keep on falling down into an abyss. With time, I am slowly getting my footing back, but I'm still not sure what I trust anymore.

How do you get your feet back on solid ground? How do you find that place of comfort and joy, that desire to be part of life once again? How do you come back to that place that shouts "I'm here, world! Watch out, here I come!"

I still don't claim to know all the answers, but I can say I have been taking life one day at a time, one foot in front of the other. Sometimes it feels like I am walking in mud or about to be swallowed by quicksand, and other moments I feel like I am walking on water. So I tread onward and I try to raise my son as best as I can. I go to work and muddle through a job about which I am no longer passionate, but it's a job I do well and it keeps food on the table—a necessary thing. One day I will move on with joy and confidence, but this is not yet the time, particularly because of the economy—again something beyond my control.

And so a year passed and somehow Kean and I made it through many, many tears, countless conversations and phone calls with family and dear friends, awkward moments with people who never know what to say, the death of my dear friend's husband Phil, going back to work, Father's Day, French Meadows Camp, purging Patrick's California home, purging our Florida home, our wedding anniversary, Kean's first day of school, Thanksgiving, Christmas, all those damn holidays, the first anniversary of his death, Kean's ninth birthday and Patrick's sixty-second. The first year was absolutely the hardest and the second year only slightly less so, and I began to wonder if I would ever again look forward to holidays or birthdays.

The second year was when I felt that every ailment was a foreshadowing of my own diagnosis. A headache was surely a brain tumor. A pain in the chest kept me in the hospital for several days with a heart monitor attached to me, only to realize I had pulled a muscle working in the garden. An irregular pap smear meant cervical cancer. I was going to die and leave Kean alone on this earth. *Who would care for him?*

Who would raise my child? My sister and I talked about this at length. She was happy to be his guardian. On some level I was relieved, but I knew I had to remain healthy. I would not follow Patrick's fate.

Kevin, Patrick's client from California, never followed through with his promise to pay for Patrick's medical bills and Kean's education. Fortunately, I had just enough life insurance to pay off these exorbitant bills, but nothing more. Here was another area in which we were unprepared for the ill-fated disease that confronted our family. I prayed to God that I would remain employed in an economy that was going from bad to worse.

We recently had a third round of layoffs at my company. Twenty colleagues, many of whom I worked with for years and who were close friends, were told they no longer had a job. Once again, I was faced with circumstances beyond my control. I felt guilty, worried, and yet relieved that I was safe for the time being. *Would it happen again and, if so, when?*

It was yet another confirmation that we cannot control many circumstances, and even when we do have some control, there are limitations. We can't control our emotions. The only thing we can control is our actions and how we respond to a situation. My emotions had been out of control for quite some time. It was time to find Vashon once again. It was time to take control of my life.

At about this time, I was introduced to the Clairvision School of Meditation. Patrick and I had meditated off and on for years, but it had never been a serious practice for me. This soon changed after I took a weekend workshop on how to "awaken the third eye." The Clairvision School teaches a meditation technique that allows you to tap into your greater self and awaken your intuition. This experience and my eventual commitment was just what I had been looking for and became the anchor I needed to help me find some balance in my life.

I don't know if I will ever really get over losing Patrick. He was the love of my life, my best friend, and the father of our child. He knew me like no other person on this earth knows me. He loved me unconditionally. We were partners in every way and life was full. I was blessed, and now he is gone.

How do you pick up the pieces and start over again? How do you remake yourself after the loss of your husband, the man with whom you were supposed to spend the rest of your life and who is no longer here. How do you raise a healthy and whole child alone? How do you take care of your child's emotional and physical needs, not to mention your own? How do you make decisions about your family and know that they are the best ones? How do you go to work every day and find purpose in what you do? How do you find joy in all that you do? How do you live each moment fully alive?

Here's how I figured it out.

CHAPTER 2

My Journey

At the time of this writing, it has been almost three years since my husband's death, one year since I began writing this story. As I reflect back on all that's transpired, I consider the ways in which I've started my life over.

How have I begun to firmly plant my feet on solid ground? With all that has happened, can I ever fully trust anything in life again? Will I ever find a place of comfort, confidence, and joy? Will I feel passionate about life ever again?

There is truth in the saying that time heals, and somehow with time I have started to heal. Somehow I have been able to go on, and I am amazed that I am able to find pieces of joy again. I hear myself laughing, and I wonder who this stranger is, the one who can laugh once again. But as much as I have healed, the pain is still present, and I wonder if the aching in my heart will ever go away.

Somehow I've established a new reality, and at times I feel guilty. But for the sake of my child and my husband who is no longer here, I had to move on. Of all people, he would want me to live and to fully live alive.

And what does this really mean, to fully live alive? How does a person reach into their soul, listen to their heart, and truly live? How do we follow our heart? How do we know if our heart speaks the truth or if it is fear teasing the mind?

I ask these questions and wonder, *How will I walk the path of truth? How will I take that first step, and where will it lead?*

This has been my prayer:

> God, I pray to you to guide me on my true path. I know not where this path may lead, but I am open to your direction and to wherever it may go. I am now ready to release the pain and suffering that is in my soul. Help me to open my heart and let my heart be my new guide. Support me in starting over and guide me along the way. God, I ask you to help me sing a new song and let it be the song of truth, my truth. Help me to fully live.

How do I start over?

Perhaps there is a formula for starting over after the tragic loss of a spouse, child, relative, or dear friend. Because of this loss, you feel hopeless and are confronted with the seemingly impossible task of coming to grips with how to face another day alone. You wonder how you will go on and how you will start to live your life once again.

Is it possible to see a better future for yourself? Can that future start now?

What if I told you I had discovered a formula that will put you on a road toward joy, even peace? What if I said there is a way to reconcile your grief and reawaken your enthusiasm for life? What if this formula came in the form of a list—a to-do list for healing after the loss of a loved one?

As I began formulating this concept, I realized that many of us are driven to create lists for many things: holidays, work, vacation, home repairs. Whether it's an item on your grocery list or a task that needs finishing at the office, we make wishes to vocalize our dreams and review the tasks to recognize our accomplishments. Me? I am a master list maker. I like to make a list each day, then check each item as I go along. It keeps me on track. So simple, so powerful. I need to be on track these days.

After you've been through the untimely death of a loved one, you realize fully that there is no real stability in life. After the shock sets in, we spend time deciding whether we can ever regain our footing, let alone our place in the world. And will we simply survive or can we ever again thrive?

The death of a loved one eradicates the notion that we have control over how our lives will proceed, regardless of the plans we've made, the work we've done. After we lose the most important person in our life, we are never again sure about any outcome. We come to appreciate that we somehow survived despite great tragedy and tremendous loss. We have endured and know we can go on, but where will we go? Will we live a bitter existence or will we carry on with fortitude and, maybe, even hope?

Some of us choose the latter and get there, in part, by beginning to plan our lives again. We do it by making lists.

During Patrick's illness and just after his death, the world I inhabited became very small. I found I could only make decisions that were necessary at the moment. I could not take in any extraneous information unless it was absolutely necessary.

In time, I started writing notes to myself that became the concrete steps I was taking to once again engage in the world. According to my notes, I was functioning despite my loss, but I was also accomplishing things that were beyond daily survival tasks. *How is this happening?* I wondered. *Am I on automatic pilot? Or is something else at play?*

I was beginning to occasionally experience pleasure again. The numbness that had enveloped me was waning, and I was able to feel joy and even a bit of peace. My son would tell me a story at the breakfast table that would make me laugh. I would overhear some of my coworkers talking and I'd smile. Or I'd find myself alone in the backyard listening to the rustle of trees in the afternoon breeze, and I'd realize that I'm okay. Somehow I am.

This diary of notes helped me understand that I was leading a seminormal life despite the intermittent sorrow and pain. Little did I know these notes would evolve into a list that I would later share with others.

Here are some of the things I wrote:

- *I went back to work Thursday.*
- *Kean and I traveled to Italy to visit my sister and her family.*
- *I installed four planter beds for our vegetable garden on the one-year anniversary of Patrick's death.*
- *I found a naturopathic physician who treated me as a whole person rather than just my symptoms.*

- *I have weekly healing sessions with my team of healers.*
- *I started exercising at the YMCA.*
- *I had the living room and family room repainted.*
- *I went through a few of Patrick's belongings and boxed up some things for Goodwill.*
- *I attended the Clairvision Meditation workshop in New York.*

These items on the list, though somewhat challenging at the time, also brought an element of satisfaction. I found that I still had an interest in decorating the house even though it was painful to change what had been familiar to Patrick and me. The act of redecorating gave me permission to express myself creatively, and in this expression, I felt a sense of freedom and independence. I was able to make my own decisions about changing the house, and I felt good about these decisions. Best of all, redecorating was fun and it gave the house a fresh, clean look.

Pondering the idea of the list, I started to pull together a variety of different types of lists to test my theory, and this is what I came up with:

Lists for Every Day

The Grocery List

The To-Do List

The Shopping List

The New Year's Resolution List

General List

The Best Seller List

100 Things to Do Before You Die

10 Twitter Lists You Should Follow

100 Greatest Songs of All Times

As I continued to ponder the idea of the list, I began to see that some lists became "how-tos." In other words, if we follow a specific list of ideas or principles, we would achieve a desired goal. The more I considered this idea the more I realized how, in every profession and area of life, there is a specified list of principles and instructions that allow us to achieve particular goals. Consider diet and exercise books. Each promises specific results if we simply follow the guidelines. Of course, easier said than done! Here are some more examples:

Lists for Health

10 Favorite Health Tips

The 12-Step Program (AA and NA)

The 101 Best Things to Do
for Your Body Now!

Top Fitness Tips

Lists for Professionals

Learn How to Draw—Step-By-Step

10 Easy Steps to Writing Well

The Sustainability List

The List for LEED Certified Homes

The Checklist for Planning a Community

Lists for Spirituality

The Ten Commandments

The Seven Chakras

The Seven Spiritual Laws of Success (Chopra)

The Seven Universal Laws

The 12 Universal Laws

The 20 Universal Laws

The 11 Forgotten Laws

Lists for Healing after Loss

The Healing Checklist

The List for Managing Your Grief

Three Steps to Take When You Are Embraced by Grief

The List of Recommended Reading for Grief

Six Steps for Managing Loss

Or how about this book:

Finding Joy After Loss: My Seven-Step Journey of Transforming Grief into Joy

What if there was a list that would allow you to start over after a devastating loss? A list that focused on ways to rediscover joy? And what if this method was simple? Could one simply follow a list of things to do to overcome grief? Was I so desperate to discover a way to find joy that I was grasping at a silly solution? Or maybe I was on to something. What if I created a formula, a step-by-step process, tested it, and found it was easy and it worked?

Okay, nothing in life is easy. Change is difficult under the best of circumstances. How many New Year's resolutions have I broken? How many times have I tried to rid myself of an old habit or to start a new one only to decide it was too difficult?

How many excuses have I made? Why would I think that this experience would be any different? But after my husband died, I found myself suffering more than I ever had. I was desperate and alone and afraid that I would not find a way out of my despair. I had to try something, anything.

Part of me was afraid of creating this to-do list. It felt too structured and confining, and yet I loved the order that it provided.

I craved a routine or a map that would provide directions to finding the old me again. Over the past three years, I had lost Vashon and I wanted to go home to her. Could this map lead me home?

Here is my first attempt at making the list, which would eventually become the seven steps to transforming grief into joy.

1. SPIRITUAL CONNECTION

Meditate

Connect with Community

Connect with Nature

Travel

2. THE APPRECIATION/GRATITUDE LIST AND JOURNAL

3. FORGIVENESS

The Forgiveness Diet

Emotional Freedom Techniques (EFT)

4. LOVE

Self-Love

Checking In

Family and Friends

Community

Helping Others and Service

Relationships

Pets

5. EXERCISE

Walking

Group Exercise/Gym

Yoga

Personal Trainer

6. HEALTH

Complete Physical

Healing

Bodywork

Eating Well

Foods, Supplements

Clearing Clutter

7. CREATIVE EXPRESSION

Imagination/Creative Visualization

Image Board

Affirmation List

Hobbies

Flowers, Garden, Cooking,
Reading, Writing

Why seven steps? Why not ten or thirteen or twenty-four, for that matter? In my research of various numbers and lists, the number seven seemed to be a constant. Seven has always had an element of spirituality to it. Seven is also considered to be a lucky number.

There are Seven Natural Wonders of the World, Seven Wonders of the Ancient World, Seven Wonders of the Middle Ages, seven days of creation, seven days of the week, seven deadly sins, seven chakras, seven senses. Seven, made up of three and four. The Pythagoreans had high reverence for the number seven. And now: seven steps to transforming grief into joy.

CHAPTER 3

The Seven Steps to Finding Joy

Think of this chapter as a map for finding your joy again; I will lead the way. For each of the seven items on my "to-do" list, I will discuss how it became a necessary step in helping to transform my grief into joy and how it can help do the same for you. Most of the steps require that you do certain things to complete them. I call these substeps. And in some cases, there are several ways to express or engage in a step. Whatever the case may be, the suggestions in this chapter are for your exploration to help you reclaim the joy you once felt. Be sure to be patient with yourself. . . . Just take it one step at a time. Of course, if you'd like to, you can do all seven steps each day, but you can also do just one or a few. It's up to you.

1. SPIRITUAL CONNECTION

Meditate

I meditated off and on throughout my life, but it was not until the death of my husband that my meditation became something that I would engage in on a daily basis. I found that meditating regularly was the one thing that I could count on to help me get through each day. There were times I would meditate several times a day, hoping that this would help to ease my pain. Meditating became my haven, my grounding rod, and my anchor.

When I meditate, I connect to God or to an energy that feels expansive, vast, and unlimited. I find that when I connect to this energy, I am not so caught up in the mundane aspects of daily life. I'm able to touch life from a place of joy and peace after my meditations. I know this all sounds cliché, but it was all I had to stay connected to this earth.

The form of meditation that I practice regularly is based on the Clairvision School of Meditation. It works on the energy centers (chakras) in the body, specifically on using the third eye as a way to awaken the self to the self.

To gain the most benefit from meditation, it is essential to practice on a regular basis. If you are not comfortable with meditating, you might want to explore other disciplines that help you connect to your higher self. Whether it is meditating, attending church or synagogue, prayer, chanting, or participating in a drum circle, try to make sure that you engage in this activity routinely and consistently.

Research has revealed that meditating for ten to twenty minutes a day increases the alpha waves in the brain and therefore decreases anxiety, stress, and depression in most people. Numerous studies document the positive effects of meditation. For those recovering from grief, a reduction of stress and anxiety is the key.

Connect with Community

During my healing process, I found it important to connect with as many groups of like-minded people as I could. I found it helpful to relate to those who shared a commonality or interest. These groups are diverse and reflect my many interests, and one group does not necessarily take precedence over the others. For example, I love my monthly Organic Growers meeting as much as I love cheering in the stands with the other basketball moms. These communities have reminded me that I am not alone; rather, I belong to a greater collective who shares a similar value system. This thought remains a comfort to me.

Community was healing for me a year after Patrick died when I flew to New York to study at a meditation school. For two weeks, we meditated, connected with God, and did emotional clearing exercises. From the growth of that experience, I now facilitate a small group that meets at my house twice a month. During our meetings, we meditate, study, and do exercises to facilitate our spiritual growth. We spend time sharing our experiences about how meditation provides an anchor in today's hectic world. The bonds I've developed with the other participants are very deep and have connected us on a spiritual level.

Shortly after Patrick's death, Kean and I became involved in a local organization called New Hope for Kids that provides counseling for children who have lost a loved one. We attended meetings on a regular basis for nearly a year. Kean grappled for some time with the fact that in his small circle of friends, he was the only one whose father had died. At New Hope for Kids, he was able to see that he was not alone in his loss. Attending this group helped support Kean and me during a critical time in our grieving process. We found acceptance and understanding in a community of friends who shared some form of the same unfortunate and too-soon loss of a loved one.

Connect with Nature

In the year after my husband died, I made a point of spending as much time as possible outdoors. I live in Florida, which, despite the brutally hot summers and possible threat of hurricanes, some people call paradise. For eight months out of the year, the temperatures are mild, the air is fresh and clear, and the vegetation is green.

I walked daily, sometimes for hours at a time, in my neighborhood, in a park, or beside one of Central Florida's many lakes. Studies have shown that exercise releases endorphins, natural pain relievers, in the brain, which counteract depression and anxiety, but I wasn't walking specifically for those reasons. I walked because it felt like the right thing to do and it somehow relieved the pain in my heart. Each day I saw flowers, heard a barking dog, watched a squirrel run up a tree, or glimpsed children playing in the yard. These observations took me out of my despair and created distractions of beauty or interest that made me momentarily forget my sorrow.

Thanks to my husband, my son and I live in a modest house that backs up to a small lake. Every day I get to watch the ducks, herons, and even the occasional hawk flying by. I watch turtles and fish swim in the water. I have the pleasure of watching my son play with his friends by the lake shore, collecting tadpoles in the spring and fishing on weekends. We have the greatest oak tree in our yard. Its branches tenderly spread out over the back lawn where my son's tree house stands. It was built by my colleagues as a gift to my son. It is his haven, like the yard and water have become mine.

Perhaps my favorite piece of earth from which I draw solace are the four raised vegetable beds, which were installed in my backyard one year after Patrick died. The planning and planting of this garden symbolize a new beginning, spiritual growth, and a simple way to nurture my body and soul. It has been such a joy to grow our own organic vegetables, and it is even more satisfying to pick them for a meal. The planting, watering, and caring for these vegetables are things my son and I enjoy doing together.

Ecotherapy, ecopsychology, and wilderness therapy are all types of therapy that help people heal by connecting with nature. Science has shown that people who spend time in nature have lower levels of the stress hormone cortisol, which is said to lower blood pressure and create greater mental health (*Green Environments Essential for Human Health, Research Shows,* Science Daily, April 26, 2011, from www.sciencedaily.com).

Travel

Since Patrick's death, I have had the great opportunity to travel domestically and internationally. The first few trips made me uncomfortable and were disorienting.

What am I doing traveling without my husband? I asked myself. *Why was he not with us? How would I figure it all out?*

Yet, despite those anxious moments, I could actually find moments of joy on these journeys. Being away from home and all its memories helped me to separate from my place of constant grief and helped me to understand that there was life outside my world that had become so small. It was during these travels that I started to appreciate again the unique beauty of a foreign country and consider all that its culture had to offer.

Kean and I were fortunate to visit my sister Fawn and her family in Italy several months after Patrick's death. My husband had acquired frequent flyer miles from his many travels. Fawn was desperate to help Kean and me, and she felt a visit with her family would be her way of nurturing us. After many encouraging phone calls, she convinced us to visit for several weeks. It was there with her that I found I could laugh again, and those moments—sitting in an outdoor café, visiting a cathedral, or eating a fabulous bowl of pasta—provided a glimmer of hope in the darkness that was our lives.

There is something affirming about the privilege of experiencing cultures and environments different from your own. Even a short trip to South Florida has the power to invigorate and nurture me. If you can afford even a modest trip, I'm sure it will help with your healing process.

2. THE GRATITUDE LIST

Appreciation is the act or expression of gratitude. It has been said that what you give, you receive back. Expressing appreciation and gratitude not only helps you to focus on the positive aspects of your life, but it also allows you to attract goodness back into your life. In times of grief, this act helps you focus on the glimpses of beauty that still exist in your life.

One of the first things I did to feel better was to start an appreciation journal. Every night before I went to sleep, I wrote down three to five things for which I was grateful. This practice helped me see that, despite all the pain, I still had things in my life for which to be thankful.

Here are a few examples of what I wrote:

- *I am grateful for my son and the joy he brings to my life.*
- *I appreciate the love I receive from my family and friends.*
- *I appreciate my cats and their unique personalities.*
- *I appreciate the flowers blooming in my garden.*
- *I am grateful for my job and the ability it gives me to make a difference in people's lives.*

The key to this exercise is to allow yourself to really feel what it is like to feel grateful. Feel the love and warmth that you receive from each of these items of appreciation. Feeling is the key to allowing more in your life.

The fascinating aspect about gratitude is that it forces you to shift your perspective. You cannot feel bad when you're feeling grateful. I started to play with this idea of gratitude, and I found that the more I focused on being grateful, the more I felt it was an invitation to allow joy into my life. I have a piece of paper on my desk that reads: "Gratitude opens the door to abundance." Can it be that simple?

My evening list has grown to include moments throughout the day when I try to remember to see the things around me for which I am grateful. This exercise helps me to be in the present and to give thanks throughout the day.

Rhonda Bryne, author of *The Secret,* wrote, "If you practice gratitude every day it won't take long before gratitude is your natural state of being, and when that happens you will have unlocked one of the greatest secrets to life."

3. FORGIVENESS

Forgiveness is the act of letting go of resentment, which can be very challenging, especially if we feel like we have been wronged. Forgiveness does not mean that we forget what has happened to us, but it does mean we are able to look at it differently. This act of letting go provides a vehicle to create more energy and joy in your life.

During the course of Patrick's illness and after his death, I noticed how it became much easier to let go of things that would have bothered me in the past. Once faced with a life-threatening illness, I clearly understood what was truly important in life. It was no longer necessary to be right or to have all the answers. What was important was to embrace my relationships and to quickly forgive when I thought I might have been hurt.

In the beginning, what is most important is to heal your relationship with the person who passed away. This can only be done when you are ready. As I was writing this, I realized I had not healed my relationship with Patrick. I was still angry with him for leaving me, but now I was ready to forgive him.

The Mayo Clinic suggests that forgiveness helps us to let go of stress and anxiety and leads to greater spiritual and psychological well-being.[1] This is something I'm sure anyone who is reading this would like to have! The following process helps make it possible:

1. *Forgiveness: Letting go of grudges and bitterness,* by Mayo Clinic staff, Katherine Piderman, PH.D. (expert), November 23, 2011, from www.MayoClinic.com

The Forgiveness Diet

The Forgiveness Diet is an amazing and very practical process that was developed by Sondra Ray, an author, teacher, rebirther, and founder of the Loving Relationships Training. I have found this technique to be a very effective and powerful process to use in situations in which I have a hard time forgiving myself or others who I felt have caused some form of emotional pain in the past.

The Forgiveness Diet goes like this: for seven days in a row, write seventy times on a sheet of paper the name of the person you want to forgive. Specifically, on the left-hand side of the paper write:

> "I ______________ (YOUR NAME) forgive ______________ (THE PERSON YOU WANT TO FORGIVE) for ______________ (THE THING YOU WANT TO FORGIVE THEM FOR)."

On the right side of the paper, write how you feel about writing down this statement.

I have tried this exercise many times, and the results were immediately startling. The first time I tried it involved a friend of mine, Laura, about whom I was feeling some resentment. After I finished the seven-day exercise, I received a phone call from Laura, out of the blue, asking me how I was doing. What was amazing was that I had not spoken to Laura in over six months. We had a lovely conversation that day and have remained good friends ever since.

You may experience a range of emotions as you work through the seven days of forgiveness. The first days, you might not feel much of a response to the person you are forgiving, and, in fact, you may find it hard to write anything at all in the response column. The next several days, you may start to feel some anger or resentment toward the person you are trying to forgive. Toward the end of the process, you will likely wonder how you are ever going to forgive this person. In the final days of the process, your anger will probably subside, and by the last day, you will feel immense love for the person you were hoping to forgive. I have found "the diet" to be a very healing and transformational process. Of course, everyone will have their own experience, and it may vary from what I have written. What has been consistent for me is how freeing and liberating the process has been. To feel freedom from resentment, guilt, shame, or anger is to feel liberated and alive again.

Once you complete this seven-day exercise, it is important to destroy the pages you have written on. You can throw them away in the garbage or better yet, you can burn them and let them go, forever.

Several days before Patrick passed away, he called the people who had been closest to him in his life and told them how much he loved them and that he held no hard feelings regarding their past relationship. I could see the love, compassion, and freedom in his face as he had these deeply intimate conversations with his family and friends. It was very liberating for him.

Emotional Freedom Technique

Emotional Freedom Technique (EFT), or Tapping, is a process that helps to release challenging emotional and physical stresses from the body. Participants lightly tap their fingers on particular acupuncture points while using specific dialogue related to the issue in order to release unwanted thoughts and beliefs.

This is how it works: Acupuncture points are specific points located along the meridian lines in the body. There are twelve main meridian lines or channels of energy, *chi,* running through the body. These meridian lines are associated with the main organs in the body. It is believed that an energy blockage or stress in one or more of these lines can cause a physical or emotional blockage. Tapping specific points can help release these stressors and cause an emotional release of energy.

I have been using EFT for some time now and have had astonishing results. I find that when I have a stressful thought and I simply tap on the thought, it either goes away altogether or it diminishes. If the stress does not completely go away, I look at a similar or related issue that may have more relevance to the issue. I then tap on the new thought and usually find that the troubling thought no longer holds the negative charge of emotion.

Just recently I felt like I was coming down with a cold. I had been sneezing and blowing my nose all day. I was concerned because we were leaving on a trip in a few days and I did not want to be sick during my travels. That night, I tapped on the thought of getting sick. When I woke up the next day, my cold was completely gone. Call it a coincidence or call it the power of tapping. I also use this technique on nights that I have trouble sleeping, and to my relief, I am finding great success with it.

4. LOVE

Self-Love

When I lost Patrick, I lost a part of myself. I became detached from my emotions because it was too painful to feel. My world became very small, and I shut down emotionally as a survival mechanism.

As I continue on the path of healing, I'm seeing that I'm more in touch with my feelings. I'm gently waking up to parts of myself that I never knew existed. It's akin to a rebirth. I'm slowly opening up to what is around me. I'm unsure of the direction my life will take, but I'm open to opportunities without judgment. Most of all, I'm trying not to feel as if I have to figure it all out.

In my need to discover my feeling self again, I began to play a game I recently invented. Each day, I would identify things with which I came into contact that I realized I liked. It started out simply:

I like the color of Sarah's sweater.

I appreciate the design of the sports car driving next to me.

I enjoyed the conversation I had with my colleague.

I appreciate the presentation of the food served to me.

Soon after I started this, I wondered if I could transform a thing I liked into something I loved if I paid enough attention to it? And could I make it become mine as well? For example:

Could the photo in a travel magazine be transformed from a simple yearning to the certainty of actually visiting the place? Could shopping, which had turned into a necessity rather than a pleasure, become joyful once again? Could eating become again an act of joy rather than a necessity for survival? Could I really taste my food and appreciate its benefit to my body?

What started out as a simple game has evolved into a process of joyful self-discovery that continues to this day.

I encourage you to start paying attention to the things that excite you, the things that you like or appreciate. When you walk through your neighborhood, which homes do you like? Which landscapes bring you joy? What inspires you and what do you find beautiful?

When you're shopping or in conversation with a friend, what is it about this experience that brings you joy? As you begin to focus on these things, you'll begin to attract more and more of these treasures into your life.

It's like falling in love. When you are open to love and start allowing love into your life, you start to fall in love with everything. It becomes contagious and expansive, and it colors every opportunity in your life.

Checking In

One of my favorite things to do each day is to spend several minutes throughout the day "checking in" with my heart, the place where I connect with my center—my true self. When I connect to my heart, I imagine sending nurturing thoughts and warmth to it.

The more I tune into this place, the more I get to know who I really am. Connecting with my heart, I find I am able to nurture and love myself. The more time I spend here, the less time I spend in self-doubt and self-criticism. The more time I am connected to my core self, the more I relinquish worries that occupy my mind.

As I continue to play with this idea, I find that my heart is more open and available to others as well. There is an element of healing that seems to be taking place. I have more compassion for myself and for what I've been through.

It's important to send yourself love each day during the healing process. Tune in to the person you were before your loss and especially to the person you are becoming. Embrace this person and send her or him love.

Here are some exercises to help you to tune into who you are:

- Write down all the special qualities about yourself.
- Write down all the things you love.
- Write down all the things that you want in your life.

My husband died. Yes, that is an awful fact. But now it's my mission to be sure that my son and I acknowledge the gift of our life and find joy. I vow that, through whatever process necessary, I will find the missing pieces of myself again. I will stop at nothing. I know that part of this process is falling in love with myself and falling in love with life again. My husband's gift will not go unopened. I am still alive, and I will live this life in complete joy regardless of my circumstances.

Family and Friends

Family and friends are an essential component to living a full life. This becomes especially apparent when healing from the tragedy of losing a loved one. I was fortunate to have both family and friends living in close proximity to our home. They were (and are) essential to my healing process and continue to this day to be a source of support and guidance in my life. Hopefully, you have support from loving people around you, but if you don't, I encourage you to reach out to local support groups available in your area. These are the people who nurtured me through my grief:

My son. Are there even words to describe the love that I have for my dear child? He is the one who taught me the true art of unconditional love. I am humbled and so blessed to be his mother. He is my joy. He is the reason I seek to become whole again.

My parents. My parents moved to Winter Park to be near our family. At the time, we felt blessed knowing that we could care for them as they aged. If only I had known how much I would lean on them during Patrick's illness and after his death. It would have been impossible to endure it all without their presence, their unconditional love, and their support. I owe so much to my parents.

My sister. Though my sister lives thousands of miles away in Italy, she continues to be a great support. She has made countless phone calls and visited many times throughout the past three years. We've also taken several trips together. Her unconditional support, her joyful spirit, her strength, and her love have helped both Kean and me in countless ways.

My girlfriends. I am so blessed to have great women in my life. They are each so different and beautiful in their own special and unique ways. They were my loving support when I thought I couldn't hold on any longer. They held my hand without question and nurtured Kean when I could not be there for him.

My friends. Not all of us have family we can depend on in a crisis situation. When my parents lived overseas and I lived on my own, my close friends became my extended family. The important thing during a crisis is to embrace support from family and friends. It's impossible to go through loss alone. Sometimes friends can ease the transition through a difficult time.

Community

In my professional life, I strive to design communities where people have opportunities to interact and engage with each other. Narrow streets, street trees, front porches, pocket parks, neighborhood schools, and village centers are just some of the design strategies I implement so that people can connect with one another. I am constantly fascinated by the variety of places that support human interaction. The corner coffee shop, the neighborhood park, and the local sandwich shop each provide these special opportunities.

As I open myself up to engaging more with people around me, I see how much community is all around me. My definition of community has expanded to include interacting on a project with my coworker; the dialogue I engage in with the local postman or the person bagging my groceries; my bimonthly visits to my hairdresser; and the interactions I have with my son's schoolteacher, to name a few.

I find that the more I open myself to friendship and to community, the more room I have to give to others, the more willing I am to share myself, and the more engaging my relationships are. I find if I make myself available, there is a greater possibility that complete strangers will become friends, even for a moment. And isn't the moment all we really have?

Helping Others/Service

I began this journey with the burning desire to put my words on paper. It was a way to process all that our family had gone through. As I continued writing, I began to feel that I am meant to share my experience with others so they might find a bit of peace during their grieving processes. It brings me great joy to share my journey with you.

Service to others remains an important component in my life. Perhaps because I am aware of those who have helped me, I offer ways to serve others. Sometimes I volunteer time, labor, nourishment, or simply words of comfort. I find that when I'm serving others, I feel better about my life.

Romantic Relationships

If you have lost a spouse or partner, you may be thinking about the prospect of dating again. You alone will need to decide when the time is right for you to embark on this new journey. Also, if you have children and depending on their age, you may need to consider the needs of your child. I have just recently begun to date, and it is scary and exciting at the same time. Though I am protective of my son, I do let him know I am dating so that he can get used to the idea that this is okay and a natural thing to do. I look forward to being in a fun and loving relationship with another truly amazing man, and I think my son does too. I will never stop loving my late husband, but I do know that my heart is big enough to love another.

Pets

Pets provide great companionship, and because of this, you

may want to consider adopting one if you don't already have one. After losing a loved one, an animal's companionship and the accompanying exercise and social interaction can be very comforting and stimulating. Also, some studies claim that pets provide their owners with wonderful health benefits. That may be true, but it's their devoted friendship that tops my list.

We have two cats in our household, Amber and Ume. They have completely different personalities and dispositions. One is full of love and the other, who has always been somewhat timid, is just beginning to open up to us. Both of them provide an outlet for our attention and love. In addition to the two cats, my son has a dwarf hamster named Sunny, with whom he is completely attached. Recently, we have started looking for a dog to add to our trio of pets. Coincidentally, as we continue to heal, we are making room for more animals and more love in our home.

5. EXERCISE

Exercise is particularly beneficial to those in the midst of the healing process. I try to exercise for at least thirty minutes, several times a week. I find exercise helps alleviates stress, my anxiety and bouts of depression, and even my troubled sleeping habits. Regular exercise has been shown to stimulate brain chemicals that may help us to feel better and more relaxed. Exercise has also been shown to be good for the heart and for keeping one's weight under control. Practiced regularly, it can also help to boost our energy level by delivering more oxygen to the body.

Generally, we fall into one of two camps regarding exercise. Some say it's the last thing they want to do *or* some will admit that exercise becomes a mode of escape. We are either immobile in our grief or cannot sit still for a minute. Either way, it's important to move our bodies in one way or another. Find the exercise that you enjoy and commit to a routine. You'll be amazed at how much better you'll feel! Remember, it is advisable to speak to a healthcare practitioner before beginning any exercise program.

Walking

Walking is my favorite form of exercise. It is simple and easy, and I can do it anywhere. I simply put on a pair of walking shoes, step out my door, and take a walk around the block or to a friend's house or down the street to the neighborhood store. I am fortunate to live in a beautiful neighborhood, so my walks are always visually enjoyable. Walking also helps to remind me to appreciate my surrounding environment and, most of all, nature. Sometimes I listen to music or a recording of positive affirmations while I walk. The combination really helps me to change my frame of mind if I am not feeling well, and I find it very uplifting.

Group Exercise/Gym

Those who prefer to exercise with others may want to join a gym or take a class or find an exercise buddy. The important thing is to listen to your body and do what feels right. Are you interested in the benefits of yoga or do you simply want the company of others? Maybe both. Be open to letting your needs evolve as you go through the various stages of your grief. It's even all right to take a day off and hide under the covers in your room. Just don't stay there.

To help me get back into better physical shape and to support me emotionally, I hired a personal trainer from our local gym. She provided just the incentive I needed to start an exercise regimen. With time, I started going to the gym on my own and experimented with yoga, Pilates, and low-impact exercise. In order to feel my best, I make a habit of engaging in some form of structured exercise two to three times a week. As my body got stronger physically, I got stronger emotionally and became more grounded.

Yoga

Yoga is the practice of blending body, mind, and spirit through a series of exercises, meditation, and breathing. In Sanskrit, the ancient language of India, *yoga* means "to join" or "unite." By uniting various poses, quieting the mind, and incorporating specific breathing techniques, yoga can help to focus your awareness and to alleviate everyday stresses. For many, yoga is a spiritual practice uniting the self with the greater whole.

6. HEALTH

Health was always an important part of our lives prior to Patrick's illness and, of course, during his illness. He counseled thousands on living a healthy lifestyle and taught people on a daily basis how to create balance in their bodies and lives. This was a big part of our relationship, and I continue to make it an important part of my relationship with myself. The definition of "health" implies "having or indicating good health in body or mind; free from infirmity or disease."[1] Let's take a good look at what it means to keep the body healthy.

Get a Complete Physical

The first year after Patrick's death, I worried that every ache or pain I had would lead to a diagnosis of cancer. Throughout the first year and a half, I was in and out of doctors' offices,

1. wordnetweb.princeton.edu/perl/webwn.

having every potential ailment checked out. I imagined I had lung, breast, or ovarian cancer, that I was having a heart attack, or that I was going blind. I do not have a history of hypochondria, and in fact, I have been extremely healthy my entire life, but after Patrick was diagnosed, I realized that anything is possible. Anyone's life can be cut short.

So you don't endure the needless trials of wondering whether or not you, too, are going to suffer the same fate as your loved one, find a doctor you trust and get a complete physical. If there is any condition troubling you, find a professional to thoroughly evaluate your symptoms. If you are not happy with your doctor, find one you can trust. I interviewed several before I found the one I now call my doctor. Most of the physicians I saw assumed I was depressed and that my symptoms were psychosomatic. It was not until I found a medical doctor who specialized in naturopathic medicine that I was able to get the attention I needed. Fortunately, I am very healthy, and I now have peace of mind that I am going to be alive and healthy for my child.

Find a doctor who understands the stressful impact of losing a loved one on your physical, emotional, and mental well-being—a doctor who can provide you with resourses for counseling, bodywork, and time off, and who understands and treats the adrenal glands. The adrenal glands sit atop our kidneys, and they release hormones that regulate our stress response, also known as the fight-or-flight response. Supporting adrenal function is important when dealing with any type of stress and especially when dealing with the grief of a loved one.

Healing

Several months after Patrick died, I sought counseling for my son and me. We are very fortunate that we found a local non-profit program that specializes in providing support for children who have lost a loved one. We met with this group on a regular basis for almost a year. It was vital to Kean's well-being to know he was not the only one who had lost a parent, grandparent, or sibling.

In addition to attending this group, I began to work with a wide variety of healers and counselors who I continue to see today. It has been difficult work, and I have shed a lot of tears as I have worked through my grief. I don't know whether I will ever truly be over the death of my husband, but I do know that I will move forward in grace and gratitude for all we shared and for what lies ahead.

Therapy is available in many forms. Find a modality that resonates with you. Make sure you're seeing a qualified professional and commit to a program that is comfortable for you and your family. Grief is an ever-evolving process that takes time, commitment, and most of all, patience to overcome. Allow yourself time to heal.

Bodywork

I'm a great believer in massage, shiatsu, reflexology, and cranial sacral therapy, as well as facials, pedicures, and manicures. Touch is healing and these kinds of therapies and services allow us to be touched in a safe and nurturing way.

If possible, treat yourself to some form of bodywork. Massage helps to relieve stress, and if you hold tension in your body as I do, massage is a great way to release those aches and pains.

Be forewarned that touch can sometimes stimulate a release of emotions, including sadness and grief. You may be surprised by what you feel after a massage. This form of therapy is said to increase the flow of endorphins in the body, which are natural mood elevators. Massage aids in circulation and the flow of *chi,* or energy, throughout the body. Like any therapy, it's recommended to get some form of massage on a regular basis to achieve the best results.

Eating Well

I have been macrobiotic for fifteen years. Patrick was macrobiotic for more than thirty years. He authored five books on macrobiotics and shiatsu massage. He also published a newsletter, counseled thousands of people, lectured, and taught throughout the United States, Europe, and Asia.

Macrobiotic means *great life* (macro: great or big, and bios: life). Together, they mean living a great life in health and longevity. The macrobiotic philosophy in the West is based on a specific way of eating. It consists of a diet of organic whole grains and vegetables, beans, nuts, fruit, and sometimes fish. If you are on a macrobiotic diet, it's best to avoid caffeine, sugar, and animal foods such as meat, poultry, and dairy products. I realize cutting out these foods could be extreme for some people, but if you abstain from these foods for a couple of weeks, you'll realize the benefit to your heath. I have witnessed and experienced greater health with this eating pattern. The improvements I saw were in blood-sugar stabilization, decreased inflammation, improved sinus function, emotional stability, increased energy, and decreased aches and pains. Among the benefits will be that sinus problems may likely go away, some allergies may be alleviated, hypoglycemia often balances itself out, and emotions may become more balanced. People react to different diets differently. What works for one person may not work for another.

When my husband was alive, macrobiotics was a way of life for our family. We believed and lived what Patrick taught—that if you ate well the benefits would be seen emotionally, physically, and spiritually. There is a simple beauty and order to this philosophy that worked for our family for a long time.

Today, the diet I follow is what we in the macrobiotic community call a *wider* diet. I still follow a diet based on whole grains, vegetables, beans, fruit, and raw nuts and seeds. But now I eat a higher percentage of live raw foods. Living in a southern climate and having access to locally grown foods allows me to eat a wide variety of fresh foods. I will occasionally eat organic grass-fed and free-range meat, poultry, and some dairy products as well. To the greatest extent possible, I try to eat organic, locally grown, and unprocessed foods. This not only supports my body, but my family, my community, the local economy, and the greater good of the world at large. My strong macrobiotic foundation generally means I never stray too far from eating healthily. At the same time, I want to broaden my palate by exploring a wider variety of foods.

Fresh, organic, locally grown, unprocessed, seasonal, and variety are the primary factors in making healthy food choices. By feeding the body nutritious and wholesome food, you nurture your body and your soul.

Some of my favorite foods and supplements include the following:

Foods

1. **Lemon juice and warm water.** Drinking lemon juice in warm water first thing in the morning helps keep people regular and helps some people have a morning bowel movement. Drinking water and staying hydrated in general is very important. You may add lemon, lime, raspberry, or cucumber to add flavor to your water. It is suggested that you take your weight and divide it in half and drink that amount in ounces every day.

2. **Green tea.** Green tea has many health benefits. It is high in antioxidants called flavonoids and has been demonstrated through research to inhibit the growth of cancer cells, lower LDL cholesterol levels, inhibit the formation of blood clots, and to possess antiaging properties.

   Green tea is a personal favorite of mine and drinking it is a morning ritual that I acquired during our travels to Japan. I steep loose green tea leaves in an earthenware pot for ninety seconds, then pour the liquid into my favorite teacup.

3. **Coconut water.** Coconut water is high in electrolytes, potassium, and vitamin C and is very hydrating. These nutrients are important in detoxification processes in the body.

4. **Juicing.** I am a big fan of vegetable juicing and try to juice at least three to four times a week. Juicing helps me to get my daily intake of raw vegetables. Vegetables are high in vitamins and minerals, and when used in juicing, help to detoxify the body.

My favorite combination of vegetables is celery, kale, broccoli stems, parsley, carrots, apple, and ginger. I now grow most of these vegetables in my garden, so quality and freshness are assured.

Vegetable Juice Recipe

1 stalk of celery

1 leaf of kale

1-inch stalk of broccoli

sprig of fresh parsley

2 large carrots

$^1/_2$ apple

dime-size piece of fresh ginger

Put all ingredients through a juicer. It is best if you drink the juice immediately to get the maximum nutritional benefit of the juice.

5. **Superfoods.** Superfoods are foods rich in vitamins and minerals. These foods are said to help fight against a wide variety of diseases as well as to slow down the aging process. Popular superfoods include acai, avocado, beans, berries, cacao, chlorella, green leafy veggies, nuts and seeds, sea vegetables, and wild salmon.

   I eat superfoods on a daily basis, and include these ingredients in special drinks and elixirs that I make several times a week. This assures me that I am getting high-quality foods rich in antioxidants, vitamins, and minerals throughout the day.

6. **Avocado.** Avocado is a fruit that is high in potassium and fiber and is a great source of healthy fats.

   I eat avocados in salads and sandwiches, or by themselves with a little salt and olive oil. They are also delicious as guacamole or with hot sauce.

7. **Brown rice.** Brown rice is a whole grain that is packed with a wide variety of nutrients, especially vitamin B and minerals. It is high in fiber, helps to reduce cholesterol, and regulates blood sugar.

   Before Patrick passed away, our family always had a pot of fresh brown rice made and ready. Daily, I would soak the rice for several hours to enhance the nutritional availability of the grain, then place the rice in an Ohsawa pot and cook it in the pressure cooker. An Ohsawa pot is a ceramic pot that fits directly inside a pressure cooker. The theory behind the Ohsawa pot is that it is better to cook your food in an earthenware container rather than directly in a metal pot. Food cooks more evenly and the flavor is enhanced by this cooking process.

There are many ways to serve brown rice, and one of our favorites was to serve it with gamashio. Gamashio is a mixture of toasted sesame seeds and sea salt, which is ground to create a condiment for rice or vegetables. I would then make a porridge with leftover rice for our morning cereal. I mixed the cooked rice with nuts, raisins, cinnamon, vanilla, and rice syrup. It is still one of my favorite breakfast meals.

Supplements

1. **Fish Oil.** Fish oil is high in omega-3 fatty acids or EPA/DHA. There are too many health benefits of fish oil to name them all here. My favorite benefits are decreased risk of heart disease, decreased inflammation, improved mood, and healthier aging of the skin and tissues.

2. **Probiotics.** Probiotics help to keep the intestinal landscape healthy, which helps maintain a strong immune system. It is well known that we have many more bacterial cells in our bodies than human cells. Therefore, it only makes sense to align ourselves with the bacteria that help keep us healthy. Probiotics are found in fermented foods, like yogurt, kimchi, and sauerkraut.

3. **Multivitamin/Multimineral.** A good multivitamin/multimineral is essential if you are not eating enough veggies. It also contains B12, which is needed if you are a vegetarian, as it is typically found in meat.

4. **Fiber.** A couple good sources of fiber are chia seeds, flax seeds, and hemp seeds. These are high in healthy fats and antioxidants, aid in colon regularity, and help balance blood sugar. Fresh vegetables and fruits, as well as beans and whole grains, are very high in fiber. If you are eating lots of these foods, you may not need to supplement your diet with fiber.

Clearing Your Clutter

I won't even pretend to be an expert on this broad and expansive topic, but I'll talk about my own experience decluttering my life. Clearing your own clutter—not to mention the clutter of a deceased loved one—can be a daunting task. Only you can decide when it is the appropriate time to let go of some of these things. When there are children involved, it can be even trickier to determine what to save and what is appropriate to let go.

I was not able to touch any of Patrick's possessions for at least a year after he died. Then I slowly let go of his clothes, toiletries, papers, and other personal belongings. When I forced myself to do this, it was wrenching to think that my husband's life could be reduced to a few boxes of possessions. There are still things of Patrick's that need to be processed, but I am patient with myself and know I will take care of these items when the time is right.

In addition to your loved one's possessions, there are your own things to purge or declutter. I find that a home filled with unnecessary possessions creates a scattered mind. If you can find the time to declutter your home, I would encourage you to do so. These days, my motto is: "If I don't love it, I no longer keep it."

Of course, you have to respect your children's possessions, and then there are the practical things you need to keep for home maintenance. I'm really talking about clothing, knick-knacks, and decorative items. If you don't love it and don't need it, let it go.

To feel good about being in my house without my husband, I had to do an assessment and really think about how I felt in each room. What did I want it to look like and how did I want to feel in each room? With time, I slowly made changes that reflected who I am now. Removing his old easy chair, the one I always disliked, made me feel a bit disloyal to my husband. But I knew I had to move on and that he would want me to have things arranged as I wanted them now.

In the past few years, I've completely repainted the interior of our house. I have framed some of Kean's artwork and hung various pieces on a wall in the family room. I bought new towels and sheets. Just recently, I replaced some of our living room furniture. These things represent the new me, my emerging identity as I learn to live without my beloved husband.

7. CREATIVE EXPRESSION

Imagination/Creative Visualization

I have always been a daydreamer. As a child, I spent countless hours in my head in one world or another. This world of imagination led to expressing myself on paper, and eventually, to a career as an urban designer. For twenty-five years now, I have designed communities of varying scales. What starts out as an idea on paper can become an actual community or town where hundreds, or thousands, of people might live.

On the flip side, spending too much time in my head can sometimes get me into trouble. I have a very analytical mind, and this can lead to picking apart even the tiniest detail. The writing of this book has led me to consider ways that I have used these tendencies to my advantage. This new understanding and my experiences of the past few years have started me wondering, *Why not start imagining my life the way I would like to see it?*

Now, folks, I'm not crazy. I can't create world peace or a dozen other things I'd like to see happen. But I might have more control over some things than I ever thought possible. Being more available to gratitude and love has allowed me to see outside the confined box in which I had been living for the past six years.

What if I could imagine living differently and what might this look like?

I started thinking about my book, and I imagined all the possible things that could be associated with it: perhaps a video series, a workbook, a made-for-TV movie! I thought about my son, seeing him happily playing with his friends and having fun at school. I thought about what it would feel like to be in another loving relationship with an interesting, caring man. I thought about my home and the traveling I want to do and so much more. This time spent imagining has now become part of my morning ritual. I spend time feeling what these things would feel like if they were part of my life. I then release these thoughts with the knowledge that they truly are my future. At the same time, I continue to be grateful for all I have right now. I believe abundance is available for everyone, and there is no limit to its supply.

Spend time daily, preferably in the morning and at night, imagining the life you want to have. What would it feel like if this (job, travel plan, relationship) were a reality? Believe that what you're feeling and seeing has already happened. Give thanks for this thought and then let it go.

> ***"Imagination is everything. It is the preview of life's coming attractions."***
>
> —ALBERT EINSTEIN

Image Board

One of the healers I worked with suggested that I create an image board. She felt it would help me rediscover the things I liked, and the images would visually be available to me on a daily basis.

For weeks, I collected words and images of things I liked. What started out as a chore became a nightly ritual that allowed me to rediscover my passions. I looked forward to discovering what I was drawn to at this time of my life, to know what made my heart sing. After I collected these images, I arranged them on a large poster board. Travel images went in the right-hand corner; decorating ideas were to the left; family, kids, and friends were at the bottom; relationships were in the lower left; and health and self-related images were in the middle. It became an art project for me, and my creative juices flowed when I thought about the possibility and reality of my future.

As I reflect back on my image board, I see that some of these images have become real. I am healthy, and my son is happy and thriving. We have had the opportunity to travel, and my home and garden continue to evolve beautifully. It has been a year since my last image board, and I am now ready to start a new one!

Affirmation List

Affirmations are statements about a desired outcome that you repeatedly tell your subconscious mind over a period of time. In order for these affirmations to become effective, they need to be repeated daily and with feeling, as if you're already experiencing these changes in your life. Cognitive experts say that it takes anywhere from thirty to ninety days to change a negative thought pattern into a positive one.

I created a list of eight primary areas in my life where I want positive change to occur. They are:

1. Spiritual Life
2. Personal Life
3. Family Life
4. Relationship with Significant Other
5. Wealth
6. Health
7. Career
8. Charity

Within each of the above areas, I created a list of at least five statements in the present tense describing what I already have. For example, under Spiritual Life I wrote: "I am daily being guided to my highest good."

I read this list at least two times a day, imagining what it feels like to have these things manifested in my life. Sometimes throughout the day I will focus on one particular affirmation and repeat it several times with feeling, to ingrain the particular affirmation at that time.

Hobbies

During your grieving process it might be a good time to take up the piano or learn how to cultivate orchards, or maybe you've always thought about learning how to paint with watercolors. Hobbies are a great way to help you engage in life again. Here are some of my hobbies:

Gardening

I have always puttered in the garden. A year after the death of Patrick, I had a raised vegetable garden installed in my backyard. To me, this symbolized a new beginning, growth, and a way to nurture myself. It's so fulfilling to cultivate my own organic vegetables, and it's even more satisfying to harvest them for a meal. This year we're growing broccoli, Swiss chard, assorted greens, kale, turnips, snap peas, leaks, and a variety of herbs. Tending to the garden is something my son and I enjoy doing together.

Flowers

As I reflect on things I love and enjoy, I have to say that flowers are near the top of my list. During this time of healing, I have tried to have fresh flowers in my house as often as possible. At least once a week, I bring in a bunch from the garden—a blooming orchid, zinnias, or any flower that is in bloom. If they are not available, I make a point of purchasing a bouquet of gerbera daisies, freesia, dahlia, or a mixture of assorted flowers. It's amazing how much I enjoy seeing them around my house. Flowers are like little blessings that come in different colors and packages.

Cooking

During Patrick's illness and after his death, it was all I could do to put a meal on the table. I was very fortunate for I have a great group of friends who provided home-cooked meals during his illness and after his death. This was their way of helping us out in a time of crisis, and I was ever so grateful.

It has taken time, but slowly I am getting back into the routine of cooking for my son and me, and I am finding that I am enjoying it as well. I'm starting to experiment with various recipes and menus and am even dreaming up a few on my own. What is especially enjoyable are the times Kean and I cook a meal together. Pancakes are no longer a breakfast item, and dinner can be eaten in front of the television, at the dinning room table, or outdoors if the weather is amenable.

To help support the cooking process and to add more variety to our meals, I have recently started to do some menu planning. It's nothing elaborate, just two to four new recipes a week that I know my son and I will enjoy. Also, I am pulling out old recipes and preparing them once more. Again, it is part of this desire to be more creative and to engage more purposefully in life.

In this way, I am providing more variety in our diet as I am preparing healthy and nutritious foods. I can always tell when Kean has enjoyed his meal. It's those times when I don't have to convince him to finish his dinner.

Reading

Shortly after Patrick passed away, I started to read every book I could get my hands on that pertained to death and the afterlife. I wanted to understand and to know where he was, what he was doing, and what it was like on the other side. When

I became saturated with the subject matter, I switched to novels. As soon as my son was in bed, I would devour one novel, then another. This was my escape to another world, one in which I didn't really have to take responsibility for my feelings. Now I read selectively, more for pleasure than information.

Find out what brings you pleasure and allow yourself to indulge in it. It will soothe the mind and nurture the soul.

So there you have it. The seven steps to transforming grief into joy. Now read on to discover how I tested, implemented, gave up, redirected, and uncovered a bonus step. Follow me on this journey of self-discovery and see how these seven steps awakened my soul and brought me back to life.

CHAPTER 4

My Progress Journal

After creating the seven steps I decided to practice them for three months and keep track of my progress and note my observations along the way. This would give me a good idea of what was working, what wasn't, and what needed to be modified. I had decided it was time to put my words to the test and to practice what I had been writing.

I asked myself the following questions: *Is it possible that following these seven steps will lead to a more fulfilling and joyful place in my heart? Can practicing these step daily and diligently transform my life from one of grief and despair to a life filled with purpose, passion, and joy? Are these the "sacred seven" or will the list need to be modified, tweaked, or even transformed to something different? Is there a formula, a secret to finding joy after the death of my husband? Or am I doomed to misery and heartache? Can my life be transformed?*

I committed myself to this three-month experiment. I decided that if at the end of three months there hadn't been a significant change in how I felt about my life, then I would extend the experiment for an additional three months or more if necessary. I planned to evaluate the degree of this change and determine whether I should continue, modify, or do something completely different. I wanted this experiment to be somewhat fluid, but I also knew it would require structure on my part.

Nothing new can be learned without commitment, practice, and a bit of structure. My son is on the basketball team. His goal is to play high school and maybe even college basketball. His coach has told him that in order to play at those levels, he has to practice specific exercises 100 times a day. Every day, Kean practices for an hour shooting baskets, fancy dribbling, and left-handed layups. As I was writing this, he was outside at 8 p.m. in 90-degree weather practicing. He'd had a long day at school. Probably the last thing he wanted to do was shoot baskets, but that's exactly what he was doing. Likewise, I knew if I wanted to reach my goal and rediscover my joy, I would have to practice my exercises daily. I was determined to do this for both myself and my son. I could do this for living a joyous life. *Isn't my joy worth that?* I thought to myself. *Aren't I worth it?*

I started this experiment by answering the eight questions in the Satisfaction Self-Evaluation Test on the next page to determine how I felt about myself and my life. I created these questions as a metric to evaluate how I was feeling about my life. I planned to answer these same questions at the end of the three-month process to determine if there had been a significant change in my life.

SATISFACTION SELF-EVALUATION TEST

Directions: On a scale of 1 to 10, rate how you feel about the following items, with 10 being the highest and 1 the lowest.

1. How satisfied are you about your personal life?	4
2. How satisfied are you about your spiritual life?	4
3. How satisfied are you about your social life?	2
4. How satisfied are you about your professional life?	4
5. Are you able to complete the goals that you set for yourself?	2
6. Do you feel optimistic about your future?	3
7. Do you feel engaged with your family and friends?	5
8. Do you feel engaged in your professional life?	3

My score of 27 (out of a possible 80) confirmed what I already knew: my life was a mess and it was lacking joy, optimism, and engagement. I needed to shift my thinking and move myself somehow from that stuck place of inconsolable heartache. (Turn to page 138, and take the Satisfaction Self-Evaluation Test for yourself to see where you stand as well. I hope you find it as helpful as I did.)

I desperately hoped this process would be the key to change. I was excited and apprehensive and couldn't wait to get started. I planned to start on Sunday, the beginning of the week, to begin charting my progress. This would be a new start for my new life. It had to be. (The following is a sampling of my journal entries along with some commentary about my experiences during this experiment.)

Week 1: September 26, 2010

Commentary: I spent my first week focusing on things that I am grateful for or that I appreciate. My typical routine consisted of spending the first few minutes of the morning and last minutes before sleep thinking about the things I am grateful for or what I appreciate in my life. My hope was that gratitude would set the tone for my day and how I sleep.

This exercise was initially very challenging because I quickly became aware that I have a tendency to focus on what I don't have, what's lacking in my life. After practicing this exercise for several days, I discovered that the more I practiced thinking about the things I am grateful for, the more I began to see how much I already do have in my life—great friends and family, and a healthy and happy son—and the better I began to feel about myself.

> In addition to the gratitude list, I spend time trying to focus on noticing things that I really like or love. It's easy to focus on my son and the beauty and wonder of nature, but when it comes to material things, I have a hard time identifying what I appreciate and seeing other positives in my life. Then I notice the book I am reading. The cup I use for morning tea. The painting in the hall. My car that starts! Soon, the list begins to grow . . .
>
> I know I need to start week 1 with the **"forgiveness diet."** I want to be sure that I'm not carrying any residual resentment or negative feelings toward my husband. Every evening, for seven days, I write down on a sheet of paper 70 times "I forgive Patrick for dying" or "I forgive Patrick for leaving me."

Commentary: At first, I didn't feel much of anything, and, in fact, I was somewhat detached from the process. But as the days progressed, I *grew* to understand that Patrick could not help being sick. He lived his life with purpose and dignity and courage. He was a wonderful man and he died.

By the end of the week I felt so much compassion for my husband that I was relieved. I was now able to let go of any need to blame him.

I now begin each morning with a warm cup of **lemon water**. I find it a refreshing and cleansing way to start the day. Also, whenever possible, I arrange fresh-cut **flowers** from the garden throughout the house. Flowers add a splash of joy to my home and they make me smile. I need to smile.

Week 2: October 3, 2010

This week, I'm spending approximately five minutes each morning thinking about the things that I love and all that I am **grateful** for. Some mornings, I wake uneasy or annoyed with my life. Some mornings, I feel sorry for myself, but I plow ahead anyway, listing the little things, hoping there will be a shift in the way I am feeling. The Cardinal on my front porch, this morning's rain . . .

By the end of this second week I am beginning to see a shift in my attitude and mood. I notice a difference in the way I interact with others. For two years, my grief had been a cloak I wore, and now I want to remove it and put it in a closet. My sorrow has sometimes made others uncomfortable, I know, and just a few weeks into my **gratitude list**, I am beginning once again to more fully enjoy the company of my coworkers. I am more relaxed in general about work. It's not that problems have suddenly disappeared or that my workload has miraculously lightened. But I am focusing on the positive, which includes the unwavering support of colleagues. This "glass half-full" mind-set colors the whole of my job experience and has made me grateful, indeed.

Commentary: I also started **EFT**, or what is commonly called Tapping, on a regular basis. Tapping is a simple but effective technique that involves lightly tapping specific acupressure points on the body to elicit an emotional release. It can be learned in a matter of minutes and can apply instant relief to stressful situations.

I continue to tap whenever I find myself in situations where I can't release an unwanted feeling or thought. During those first few weeks of this experiment, I found I needed to tap several times each day. I would tap to and from work and usually some time during the day. I always felt calmer afterward.

I make a conscious effort to spend more time outdoors. I walk in my yard and along the lakefront, and coincidentally, it is the time of the year to prepare our fall vegetable **garden**. It feels good to be digging in the dirt again and working on a home project in which Kean and I are both involved.

Commentary: That first week we planted broccoli, kale, and a variety of lettuce, and we took turns keeping the soil moist during those first weeks of growth.

Week 3: October 10, 2010

The weekly **meditation** group that I started a while back is really starting to gel. Maybe it is the welcome relief of the cooler weather, but as group leader, I feel calmer and more able to lead. Is my awareness of gratitude having an effect on my attitude? On the overall quality of my life?

My **gratitude list**, which I now practice first thing in the morning and last thing at night, is becoming longer, more realized, and meaningful. I am grateful for the birds at my feeder. The man at the deli who carefully wraps my fish. Then there is the unexpected visit from a friend and a shared meal. I've begun to write things down instead of simply saying them in my head. For some reason, the act of writing words on paper (and sometimes on a laptop) gives them more weight and significance. I now carry a notebook in my purse to jot down every feeling of gratitude I have. I don't want to miss anything and I want to be mindful of the smallest detail.

My morning ritual has morphed from a couple minutes of feeling grateful to spending fifteen to thirty minutes **visualizing** what I want my life to look like. For instance, I see my book project finished, realized, and for sale in a storefront window. I envision my son happy, healthy, and thriving. I visualize our family traveling the world and experiencing new and exciting adventures—maybe an African safari! For fifteen to thirty minutes a day, I can imagine a beautiful future for our family. This gives me hope. I need to feel hopeful.

Commentary: I noticed a significant shift in week 3 with the addition of the creative visualization exercise. I think that starting weeks 1 and 2, in which I focused on love and gratitude, allowed the creative visualization process to take hold more easily than if I had jumped directly into this process. Week 3 pulled all three pieces together in such a way that I began to see that it's possible to have what I want in my life. I have so much gratitude for this process.

Thursday

Sadly, seven people were laid off at our company this week. In the past, I would have felt vulnerable and wondered if my name would be on the list for the next round of layoffs. Instead, I feel compassion for my coworkers and I know that I will be okay no matter what happens next.

Week 4: October 17, 2010

I'm feeling quite uncertain and fearful since the layoffs. I'm trying to stay focused on the **gratitude** exercises and **tapping**. Both of these seem to help take the edge off these negative feelings but I'm still worried. Will I be laid off and if I am, will I be able to support us? Are we going to lose our house and how will I find a new job? Who will hire someone at my age? I'm feeling scared and vulnerable.

Gratitude, gratitude, gratitude!

Week 5: October 24, 2010

Sunday

Week 5 brings something I haven't felt in a while—spontaneity! Somehow the structure of the list seems to encourage a freedom to be open that feels foreign to me. This morning I switched up my usual Sunday routine and traded in my newspaper reading for a bike ride. Today, I'm wondering why things have to be done a certain way. Why can't I be open to what feels right in the moment? As Kean and I head out on our bikes, I wonder what change, what surprise will be next. We ride fast, pedaling around the lake. The sky is blue. What a beautiful day for a bike ride. Does this newfound spontaneity have anything to do with the seven steps?

Thursday

I have a confession to make. I'm afraid this list idea might be a ridiculous experiment on my part. What if I go through this process and nothing happens? What if these changes are temporary and I end up slipping back to feeling sad and lost?

What if this fails, and if it does, what next?

Commentary: Back to structure . . . I decided to chart my progress. I was determined to have tangible results by the end of the year. In order to follow my progress, I needed to keep track of what I was doing and consider areas I could be avoiding. I created an Excel spreadsheet with each of the seven items and subareas listed. My goal was to follow at least 60 percent of the list during each week. If not, I would amp up any areas that might have been lagging behind.

Week 6: October 31, 2010

Kean and I are traveling to Washington, D.C., to visit friends for the week. Though I'm very excited about the trip, I'm also feeling melancholy. The last time I was in D.C. was with Patrick in April of 2005. We were attending the PCRM, Art of Compassion Award Ceremony, where Patrick's dear friend, Mary

Morgan, widow of Dr. Spock, was presenting the Benjamin Spock Award for Compassion in Medicine to Dr. Esselstyn of the Cleveland Clinic.

Commentary: Patrick had been in excruciating pain during our trip to Washington, D.C. He finally shared some of his symptoms with a doctor friend, David, who insisted that Patrick see a physician when we returned to Orlando. A week later, Patrick received his diagnosis of prostate cancer. Two weeks later, he had his first operation.

Yes, there is sadness in this visit, but with the sadness is the excitement I feel in wanting to share this great city with my son, and the desire to create new memories filled with joy and laughter and discovery. No, I will not erase the memories I had with Patrick, but I will make room for new ones that include my son.

Week 7: November 7, 2010

Monday

And so we created new memories and in those new memories are feelings of joy and inspiration from all of our adventures, spending time with friends, and the chance to visit a truly inspiring and beautiful city.

We were the perfect tourists visiting the museums, monuments, and the National Mall. Of course, a trip to the National Zoo was a priority, and to top off our visit, we took the subway or trolley whenever we could. Our evenings were spent with old friends as we rested our happy but weary feet.

Thursday

I have been having a couple of "off" days. I'm less perky, less positive than I've been this past month. Is it simply the blues after our wonderful trip, or am I in a slump? I'm also beginning again to question this experiment, wondering if I need to change it up and what that might look like if I did.

On the other hand, I continue to work with my seven steps, though not with the same gusto I started with. Despite this funk, strangely small miracles are happening—more than your average mini-miracle: perfect seats on the airplane, both to and from D.C., despite no prior seat assignments; a flawless visit to a major destination city despite my travel woes; I was late to work and then my client canceled, so I wasn't late after all. As isolated incidents, they would seem like nothing that special, but together they feel more significant. I guess what I'm saying is that despite my funk, good is starting to happen in my life. Or has good been there all along and I am just beginning to take notice? Isn't perception everything? My seven steps have a power all their own and are somehow creating an impact on my life.

Week 8: November 14, 2010

Monday

It is week 8, and I'm feeling a little embarrassed that this whole experiment has been a total flop. It's stupid and silly, or maybe I'm just overwhelmed today. Maybe it's hormones, or fear, whatever you want to call it. I'm calling it failure, wondering why I believed these seven steps would lead to anything of significance. Is it a game I'm playing with myself before I face the fact that I'll never get over the loss of my husband

and maybe I never should? I'll never know joy again and that's just the way it is.

I'm going to take a break. No writing, no list keeping, no tallying things. I'm going to do nothing and see what happens. So until week 9, good-bye lists. Hello, trash TV!

Friday

A dear friend came for a visit yesterday and commented later that her twelve-year-old daughter noticed how different I seem. I looked happier, younger, she said. In fact, they were both wondering if I was in love! I laughed. After they left, I wondered if my steps were responsible for the apparent changes in me that others were seeing. Hmmmmm. Did it have anything to do with the seven steps?

Week 9: November 21, 2010

Sunday

I found it very difficult not to follow the seven steps last week. The routine has become ingrained, and these steps are encouraging me to feel grounded and more aware.

Commentary: So, no, I did not abandon the program as I threatened to! My overwhelmed feelings lasted approximately twenty-four hours, and I chalked them up to simply living life. Hopefully these tools and the company of good friends, a good movie, a wonderful read, or sometimes just a good night's sleep will get us through an especially difficult day.

When I reviewed my list, I realized some of my tenets had been practiced religiously, some only occasionally.

It's time to reevaluate things and perhaps challenge myself to commit to doing some exercises on a more regular basis. Here is what my list looks like:

Things I Do Regularly:

- Connect with my spiritual community
- Make gratitude lists
- Practice Tapping
- Notice the love of family and friends
- Go to healing sessions
- Eat well
- Take nutritional supplements
- Creatively Imagine
- Garden
- Keep fresh flowers
- Write

Things I Do Occasionally:

- Meditate
- Spend time outdoors
- Travel
- Exercise
- Juice
- Declutter
- Cook
- Read

There are five areas that I feel I can start incorporating into my routine on a more regular basis: meditating, exercising, juicing, cooking, and being more creative.

Here is my plan:

Meditation: Commit to mediating daily for fifteen to thirty minutes.

Exercise: Commit to exercising two to three times a week.

Juicing: Commit to drinking fresh vegetable juice at least three times a week. The goal is to increase this practice to daily to get fresh, raw, and organic veggies into the system.

Cooking: Be more proactive in planning fun, interesting, and healthy foods for my son and myself.

Image Board: Revisit this exercise. It's a good way to remind me of the things that I love and make necessary updates.

Wednesday

It's the day before Thanksgiving, and I'm feeling totally down and depressed. The holidays are ahead. God, I so want my husband back. Damn it, Patrick, why did you have to die?!

There are so many memories I want to erase from that time in my life, and yet they are so vivid in my mind. At times it's just a mere reflection, and other times, like today, the images feel so alive and real—haunting me.

I'm feeling vulnerable at work as well, once again wondering if I'll lose my job, questioning my capabilities as a professional.

And I'm feeling vulnerable again about the merits of this program, wondering if my list is a way to take control of my outside environment so I can comfortably live within myself.

What do I do with this list and how do I use it to work for me now? How can it help me feel good? In a deliberate attempt to feel better during this especially sensitive time, I'm listing specific action steps to be taken by me. I have decided to reach out to friends, make sure I exercise, write in my book, express my gratitude, tap, create an affirmation list, visualize a positive future for myself, and have a healing session. I have a lot on my plate, but I'm committed to feeling better despite my grief. I know it's normal to grieve, especially at this time of the year, but I also want to find some joy in between my sorrow.

Friends: Reach out to my support group, my friends, who understand my struggle and who will nurture me.

I talked to two very special friends on the phone today and one reminded me of the trip my son and I took to Morocco in April to celebrate my sister's fiftieth birthday. I was feeling very uncomfortable about our travels to what I perceived was a third-world country. I was especially concerned about sanitation and whether or not we might get sick. I prepared, researched, and purchased every known natural antibiotic and antibacterial medicine I could put my hands on, and had it neatly tucked away in our suitcase. When we arrived in Marrakech, we found out that the airlines had lost our luggage. For a solid week, we were without clothing, toiletries, and all our medicine. Fortunately, I was able to borrow some clothes from my sister, and we purchased a few articles of clothing for Kean. Needless to say, we did not get sick during the entire trip, and to top it off, the day of our departure we were notified that our luggage had been found. After picking up our bags at the airport, we were thrilled to find everything intact—medicine, birthday presents, and all. I had to remind myself that not all losses indicate disaster. Sometimes things do turn out all right.

Exercise: Go to the gym and exercise.

Write: Write in my book and express my feelings on paper.

Gratitude/Appreciation List: Write a list of things that I am grateful for and really feel what it's like to have those things in my life.

This is one of Neale Donald Walsh's quotes for the day. It is timely and very appropriate:

> *On this day of your life, dear friend, I believe God wants you to know . . . that gratitude in advance is the most powerful creative force in the universe.*

Most people do not know this, yet it is true. Expressing thankfulness in advance is the way of all Masters. So do not wait for a thing to happen and then give thanks. Give thanks before it happens, and watch energies swirl!

To thank God before something occurs is an act of extraordinary faith. And that, of course, is where the power comes from. It's Thanksgiving Day in the U.S. Why not make it Thanksgiving Day in the hearts of people everywhere, all the time?

Tapping: Continue to tap on various issues.

Affirmation List: Read my affirmations out loud and with feeling.

Creative Visualization: Imagine what the next few days will look like and how I will feel during this period of time, and then move into the future. I start this exercise in the present tense and say it out loud.

Cut out photos of favorite magazine images for visualization box.

Healing: I have a healing session scheduled with one of my therapists in two days. The theme of this session and the next few days is to face my vulnerability, face the chaos in my life, reach out to my friends, and to quit running away from the pain in my heart. I'm already starting to feel better. Knowing that I'm taking some very active steps to care for myself is already helping me to let go of some of my pain and anxiety.

Week 10: November 28, 2010

During Thanksgiving dinner, while everyone is digging into turkey and cranberry sauce, while glasses are being clinked and plates scraped later in the kitchen, I feel a wave of sorrow for the loss of my husband, for the life I once had. Will I ever be completely done with these feelings of sadness, anger, and grief?

Here I am, facing another Christmas alone. And then there would be the anniversary of Patrick's death, our son's birthday, Patrick's birthday . . . I vow to be especially nurturing to myself during this time, and reach out to friends, family, and needed resources.

Thursday

I'm feeling exhausted this week. Did the impact of Thanksgiving throw me off, or is something else going on? I'm feeling a lot of self-doubt these days, questioning this whole process, wondering where it's going.

The holidays remind me that I am alone, that my husband has died and my son and I are left to mend ourselves on our own. It's the new normal as they call it. It really is a joke when you think about it. What is normal anyway? And will our lives ever be "normal" again? We go through the actions, do all the "right" things. Kean is in school. I'm working. We socialize with family and friends. Outwardly, we seem to be coping and sometimes we are.

Then sometimes in the garden, I'll look up at the sky and realize I haven't thought about Patrick in an hour. And that's when I feel so alone in my grief.

And Kean, sweet little Kean, who is all child, is so excited about Christmas and wanting to decorate the tree, the house, and the yard. And everywhere I go there's Christmas music and decorations and invitations to come to so-and-so's party. And I smile and tell them maybe, maybe . . .

It's almost three years since Patrick died and there isn't a day that doesn't go by that I do not think of him. I drive by the hospital where he spent his last days. I hope to never step foot in that place again. It was the emergency rescue team, who came to our house at 3 a.m. to transport him, that I value. I hold those men in grace for what they did, and at the same time, my heart breaks for what they were sent to do. Those days remain etched in my memory, his body failing before my eyes. My husband and my best friend—where are you now?

Week 11: December 5, 2010

I have decided to ramp up my **healing** sessions this month. I'm going to open myself up to more self-love and meet weekly with my Clairvision teacher to work on specific issues around Patrick's death and healing my wounded heart. Can I tune into how I feel without judgment to see if there are opportunities to look at things in a different way? Can I acknowledge the wound in my heart and still be open to love in whatever form it takes?

Week 12: December 12, 2010

I'm pushing myself daily to stay centered and balanced, to feel part of this world. This week I'm entrenched in survival mode, afraid to let go. And if I do fall apart, what will happen to me? To Kean?

How do you start over after your husband dies? Yes, I'm doing all the right things, going through the motions. It all looks good from the outside, but am I living fully? Am I engaged in life? Am I really feeling part of this world?

How do you keep your heart open despite the pain?

Wednesday

I had some **bodywork** the other day, and my therapist asked me what I did to have fun. Afterward, I realized two things.

1. I have very little fun in my life.

2. Why isn't FUN on my list of Finding Joy after Loss?

Fun. How could I have missed this? It seems obvious now. Isn't fun a means to finding joy? Fun, a three-letter word—short, sweet, and yet so powerful. Could I have some fun? Could I allow myself to have fun, and would it be okay if I did? If I don't, how will I ever find joy?

Perhaps my list is all wrong. I need to rethink things. What else has been left off this list? Is it right (whatever that means) that the grieving have fun? Can I give myself permission, and what does having fun look like? I don't remember!

I talked to a friend at length about this very subject today, and she said I was being too hard on myself. I am fun to be around, she says. I liked hearing that, but she doesn't know that I feel like an actress most of the time. I pretend to be enjoying myself when I'm often not. Right now, "fun" seems like a lot of work, and I want it to be a natural expression of myself. Maybe I am expecting too much after only three years. Is there a moratorium on grief, a timeframe when life feels normal again? If I follow the list will I begin to feel normal? Or is that a concept that no longer applies?

Today somebody said that when you change the way you look at things, the thing itself changes. If that's true, is there a way to look at grief differently? And if there is, do I want to consider this possibility? Could I consider the joy of Patrick's life a gift rather than the sorrow of his death? My therapist says the other side of grief is joy. I like that. Joy. I'm ready to become acquainted with the other side of grief. I'm ready for joy and I have a feeling this gift starts with fun.

Thursday

Today, my son suggested buying Christmas and birthday presents for his father. We laughed as we discussed what he might like these days. A new scarf? *Did angels wear scarves?* we wondered. Kean went off to his room, and I put the kettle on and waited for it to boil. After a while, I poured hot water into a cup and dunked the tea bag up and down, up and down. Peppermint. It smelled good. I smiled. There it was. Joy.

Friday

I don't know where I got the idea about a grief timetable, but it's been three years since my husband's death. I'm feeling as though I shouldn't be sad anymore. How long is an appropriate time to mourn? A year? Three years? Forever?

I have been so hard on myself, feeling sad and depressed and not more engaged in the holiday festivities. Most everyone I know finds this time of year stressful. Why should I feel any differently?

Today I've decided it's possible and okay to feel sad, even depressed, and at the same time, experience joy. Kean and I talked about putting up a Christmas tree and—although it was not a great day—in that moment, I felt happy and hopeful. I've given myself permission to feel these sometimes contradictory feelings. It's what it is. My guess is even if my husband had not died, it would be the same. I have to sometimes remember to take off my rose-colored glasses when I consider how things could have been if Patrick had lived. There's no denying the occasional bad day, regardless of circumstance.

Week 13: December 19, 2010

It's week 13 and I've decided to continue this experiment for another three months. How would I rate myself? And can I say there has been progress and perhaps transformation in finding my joy?

After three months of consciously and diligently working toward this goal, I would definitely say that I feel more engaged in my personal and professional life. Despite the emotions associated with the holidays, I do feel more balanced, connected, and optimistic about life and about my future in general. Prior to this process, I could not see beyond my immediate needs, and today I have a much clearer vision about what the future may hold. I started this effort from a place of fear and uncertainty, and now I can honestly say I feel more positive. I have more joy in my life. Of course, it's possible I would have become less sad with only the passage of time. But I believe my conscious effort has expedited this quest for joy and set the stage for its arrival in my life. I had not realized how much I have transformed in these past three months until I took time to reflect. I'm grateful for this process, and I look forward to seeing how it continues to evolve in the next few months.

Now it is time to reevaluate, reassess, and rethink what's

working and what's not, and determine if anything needs to shift and change.

There are two areas I need to incorporate into my routine. I vowed to do these things more regularly when I took inventory weeks ago, but I have been remiss. From now on I will:

Meditate–daily meditation, fifteen to twenty minutes each morning

Exercise–two to three times per week

I'm wondering if had I exercised and meditated on a regular basis, then would I have been more centered this past month? It's time to make this a priority.

There is another area I realize is missing from my life and because of it I have decided to amend my list to include the **Bonus Step**. The bonus step is FUN and advocates having one fun activity per week.

Dictionary.com defines fun as: 1. something that provides mirth or amusement. 2. enjoyment or playfulness. The bonus step is going to be a bit more of a challenge for me, and this is exactly why it has to be included. I need to challenge myself to break the pattern of my grief, and quite simply, it is time to have more joy in my life. What does fun mean to me, and can I and will I allow myself to have fun? Maybe I'm really having some fun times and I don't even realize it? Time to keep track and pay attention to how I'm feeling.

Right now there are several types of fun I can identify:

Fun with my son and/or friends: goofy, crazy, silly, uninhibited fun. This type of fun is probably the most intimidating type of fun for me.

Fun with my friends, family, and/or coworkers: laughing, joking, fun with my peers. This is probably the most common type of fun I currently have.

Fun activity: adventuresome fun may include something new, different, or something I don't commonly engage in. This fun will require me to open myself up to new ideas and opportunities. Time to go outside of my comfort zone.

Week 14: December 26, 2010

I dreamt of Patrick last night. In my dream, I saw him in a bookstore with another woman and her two children. I was so angry at him for leaving Kean. How could he leave our son for another family?! When I tried to confront him, the woman and children disappeared. And then I woke up and the dream faded away.

After Patrick died, I used to dream of him leaving me for another woman or just because life was too much for him. I must now be trying to work out why he left our son. Oh, the mysterious mind, constantly trying to work things out.

Week 15: January 2, 2011

Happy New Year!

This week I'm writing down goals for 2011. What do I want to achieve in all areas of my life? What do I want my life to look like (**creative visualization**) and how will I go about achieving these goals? As I continue to delve into these different areas, I recognize my dreams and aspirations. Again, it makes sense to write things down, see them on paper or the computer screen, list each goal, figure out how I am going to achieve the goal, bring it to life. These goals are no longer thoughts floating around in my head but concrete ideas that I will put into action and bring to life throughout this year. It feels good to say that to myself and to put these words on paper.

As I was musing about the bonus step and the idea of having **fun**, I started looking around my house to see if my home reflected this idea. Do the rooms in my house reflect a sense of aliveness and playfulness? My living room, family room, and kitchen are done in earthy colors, tones that support a need to go inward and nest. For years, my home has been simple, orderly, and Zen-like.

As I prepare for the new year, I feel a desire to switch things up a bit. Perhaps these rooms will become a little less Zen-like, less orderly. What would it be like to paint a room red? Turquoise?! To lean art against a wall, like I saw in a magazine, instead of hanging it on the wall? I want to feel the joy of the unknown and take a few (color) risks. How will my home reflect this new me? Time to play with these ideas and see what emerges.

Week 16: January 9, 2011

I have been thinking a lot about **relationships** and what it would mean for me to be in one again with someone who I could open my heart to without the fear of being hurt. I'm thinking about the idea of trusting enough to allow myself to love again. I long to love again and feel that joy once more. I'll think about this as I begin the new year and maybe soon expand my definition of fun to include, well, men.

Wednesday

It hit me today that the purpose of this journey, the journey of writing this book and doing these exercises, was to reach a specific destination: the place of joy. What if the journey is the joy? Aren't all these steps a means to being more present, a means of engaging in life, if only for a moment, but in that moment it allows you to connect to one's joy? Strung together, these moments create a pathway or journey of sorts to living your life right now.

> ***"Focus on the journey, not the destination. Joy is found not in finishing an activity but in doing it."***
>
> —GREG ANDERSON, FOUNDER OF THE AMERICAN WELLNESS PROJECT, 1964

Friday

Clear your clutter. Why do I always go through Patrick's belongings right around his anniversary date? Old files, papers, bills to be shredded and discarded seem to surface at this time: another layer of his existence, another layer of memories, his notes jotted here and there on pages. What to hold on to? What to finally let go?

Saturday

I had a **massage** today—nothing out of the ordinary except that I chose to have a massage by a male masseuse. I thought it would be good for me to be touched by a man. Therapeutic, I told myself, though I had a hard time enjoying myself. Extreme feelings of sadness came up for me as he touched me. I longed to be with my husband, to be touched again by Patrick.

Yes, I do long for the day when I can be intimate again with a partner, whether it be through shared conversation, a fun outing, a meal together, or—yes—being lovingly touched.

Week 17: January 16, 2011

It's the anniversary of Patrick's death. Oh, how I remember this week. I can't quite recall specific moments so much as the overall feeling of not wanting him to suffer anymore.

I remember holding my dear child, trying to explain that his father was dying. My dear child, how my heart still aches for his pain.

Recollections of Patrick spiral through me: they are sweet, sometimes sad, and, in a flash, I am angry. If only it was Wednesday and I'd somehow gotten through the anniversary of his death yet again. It would be over for another year.

Tuesday

I went to bed last night considering how to make today a time I wouldn't dread. What could I do that would make this day positive rather than painful? What if I focused on how **grateful** I am to have had this amazing man in my life for as long as I did? What if I saw the gift of our time together rather than focused on what was lost? Could I revel in the beauty of our relationship rather than focus on his illness? Could I be sad he's gone, yet glad because I had twelve amazing years with him?

I woke up today feeling just this way. Had I not known Patrick, I would have not had my son. And how blessed I am to have this amazing child!

I'm not saying that I did not have moments of difficulty today. But between **meditating, EFT,** focusing on **gratitude**, and spending time connected to my **heart**, I was able to move relatively smoothly through the day.

Wednesday

Happy Birthday, my sweet child!

Death yesterday, birth today. Is the universe a jokester or is this juxtaposition of events a simple reminder about the push and pull of life's events?

Week 18: January 23, 2011

Time to breath.

Time to rest.

Take stock.

Tune in.

Locate peace.

Feel my **heart**.

Find me.

Week 19: January 30, 2011

I spent the entire week **tuning in to my heart**. For me, this meant not having any agenda. It meant spending time, as much as I possibly could, being fully present and in the now. It meant letting go, listening to myself, and being okay with whatever I was feeling. Although it was challenging at times, it felt good to honor however I was feeling. And in this letting go and being present, I found myself nurturing a part of myself that had not been nurtured in a very long time.

Week 20: February 6, 2011

I can now finally say that I'm able to start my day with a twenty-minute **meditation**. I have noticed that this discipline helps create an inward sense of stability and balance that fortifies me throughout the day. On days when I don't meditate, I notice an immediate difference in my sense of ease and even the level of stress that I feel. It's almost as if it gives me a boost in my self-confidence. I feel as though I can handle whatever the day may bring.

This is also the week I've gotten back to working in the garden. I'm out until dark, tilling the soil, spreading mulch, and putting in rows of plants. This year, Kean and I are planting broccoli, kale, string beans, cucumbers, lettuce, and some flowering annuals. It's lovely to watch things grow again.

Week 21: February 13, 2011

Monday, Valentine's Day

As I continue the process of **"checking in,"** I notice how more and more I am aware of my feelings that sometimes change—almost in an instant. These last few years, my emotional life has been somewhat stagnant. Things were black or white. I was sad or happy and there was little in between.

Now, I'm on a bit of an emotional roller coaster. I can be happy one minute, then sad the next. Or I can be angry in one moment, and in the next moment, laugh at something that amuses me.

What's different is that I'm beginning to be okay with all of it. I'm starting to see things on multiple levels. I can and will feel it all. It's a little like the wall in my family room where the artwork is no longer hung up in linear, predictable, neat rows. I now have pieces of all sizes and colors. Nothing goes together, and yet hung together the collection somehow works. I'm hoping it's the same with my life.

And so, on Valentine's Day as I **check in with my heart**, I wonder whether or not my heart is open or closed to the thought of another love. Thinking of Patrick can be painful and yet I'm okay with this now. I can miss Patrick and still consider the idea of a new love.

I'm slowly beginning to realize that pain is part of life and it will be for as long as I live. It may take on another form or the intensity may change, but it will be there, just as memories of my husband will always be present.

Helen Keller said, "What we have once enjoyed we can never lose. All that we love deeply becomes a part of us."

Week 22: February 20, 2011

Tuesday

Yesterday, something happened that pushed my buttons, made me angry, and ultimately got me questioning my efforts of the last six months. I had to actively do something if I wanted to feel better. So here's what I did:

Tapped

Spent time in **gratitude**

Spent time **imagining** what I want my life to look like,
and finally,

Spent time tuning in to my **heart**

I went to bed feeling better, but I had a restless night and woke up worried again. I continued with the same series of steps and soon began to feel some release. By the next day, I felt so much better. What I saw initially as an obstacle turned out to be an opportunity to work out a personal issue. These simple steps allowed me to examine an experience and consider it in a new light in only twelve hours. Thank you STEPS!

As I continue to reflect, I see that much of this personal growth is about letting go and trusting that my life will once again be full. I'm acknowledging that it is already full in so many ways. And when disappointment or sorrow or hurt come my way, I will endure and it will pass. I have so wanted to control my environment, hoping I would never have to go through the pain I felt when I lost my husband. But there is no insurance against heartache or loss. There is only the knowledge that we can tolerate a whole lot more than we ever thought possible. And in time, with love and with a few (seven + the bonus step!) simple steps, things do get better.

Week 23: February 27, 2011

It's week 23, almost six months after I started this step journey. Below are the new results from the same questionnaire I completed when I started this process.

1. How satisfied are you about your personal life? 8 (4)
2. How satisfied are you about your spiritual life? 8 (4)
3. How satisfied are you about your social life? 7 (2)
4. How satisfied are you about your professional life? 7 (4)

5. Are you able to complete the goals that you set for yourself? 9 (2)

6. Do you feel optimistic about your future? 8 (3)

7. Do you feel engaged with your family and friends? 8 (5)

8. Do you feel engaged in your professional life? 8 (3)

Wow! Is it possible that my level of satisfaction has gone from 27 points to 63 points? Have I really accomplished what I have set out to do? Have I achieved the results I was looking for? Have I found my joy?

Week 24: March 6, 2011

It's week 24, six months after I started this process. As I was mulling over the seven steps and bonus step in Finding Joy After Loss, I realized how each and every step is about **self-love** and nurturance. These steps provide me with a blueprint, a process for working through my grief that has allowed me to reconnect with my world, both physically and spiritually.

Here is a quote by Neale Donald Walsh:

"On this day of your life, dear friend,
I believe God wants you to know . . .
. . . that happiness and joy comes to you when it moves through you. There is no other pathway—and that's the miracle."

Commentary: This journey has been about finding my way back to joy after the death of my husband. It has been a prescribed journey with the premise that if I followed these specific steps I would reach a certain destination.

During this process I've realized it's not about reaching a specific destination; rather, it's the journey along the way that's important. To be able to embrace each day, give thanks for the ordinary, and to find joy in the moment is to begin to awaken to life. Patrick has given me all this.

Certain steps have allowed me to regain my self-confidence, feel more empowered, and embark on a path of self-discovery.

At different times I was not able to follow all seven steps at once. Three to four steps seemed to be my daily average, but these would vary depending on my needs. At times, I would practice several steps consecutively for weeks; other times, I would move on to some of the other steps. I would sometimes reach out for a step that I had not considered in a while only to find immense relief when I did.

I have fallen in love with each of these steps as I hope you will, too. Each has their own power, and done together allow for great energy and power. These steps are now part of my quest for a better life.

They have somehow led me to me, and in that finding, I have found my joy. I wish the same for you.

Week 40: July 2011

I have been practicing my steps to joy for nine months now, and as I reflect upon my journey, I see how these steps have helped to transform my life. And through this transformation, I can honestly say I found my joy.

What seemed like a silly, somewhat desperate experiment, continues to have the power to transform the way I feel about life after the loss of my husband. It colors how I will view my life from now on.

During the first few weeks of this experiment, I documented every step of this process. In time, the steps became part of who I was—who I am today. Now my meditation, Tapping, and gratitude awareness are as routine as morning tea. Yet, I still marvel at their power, their ability to help me stay balanced in this hectic world. Exercise and diet are essential components to my feeling balanced and healthy. Reaching out to friends and my community keeps me feeling engaged and connected with others. And let's not forget fun.

I feel like I am moving to a place of grace, and I'm happy to be here. My heart continues to open to love, and that's a good thing. I'm sure Patrick is looking down from wherever he is and is nodding his approval.

And now I encourage you to use these seven steps and the bonus step, and maybe even modify them as you see fit. Find what principles work for you and commit to them for at least three months. Be patient with yourself and have the confidence to know that those first steps will take you in the right direction.

Have courage, persevere, and be nurturing to yourself along the way. I wish you many moments of joy in your future.

CHAPTER 5

Reflections

Merriam-Webster defines joy as:

a. The emotion evoked by well-being, success, or good fortune or by the prospect of possessing what one desires: delight

b. A state of happiness or felicity

c. A source or cause of delight

In a documentary film, George Lucas said, “Taking care of others is joy.”

What is my definition of *joy?*

As I contemplate the concept of *joy,* I realize that, for me, joy is about feeling connected to God. When I am connected, I feel closest to God, and this is what brings me joy. In writing this book, I discovered that the project was really about how to connect to God in seven sacred ways, plus a bonus step. In connecting to God, I find myself.

Having this revelation, finding that *joy* is really my sacred connection to God was like discovering a hidden secret. Would I discover more if I could understand *joy* even more? Could I feel God even more? I knew my way to knowing God more was to get to know *joy* more. How could I really discover the secrets of *joy*, and could I really get to know her? Could I invite *joy* into my being so that it was no longer outside of myself, but something that exuded from within. Could *joy* and I become friends? Could we share an intimacy that was life changing and forever lasting. Could *joy* and I be the best of friends?

I decided to invite *joy* in. My morning meditation and evening prayers are dedicated to *joy*. I sit in contemplation and my focus is on *joy*, and I open up to what she might tell me. What does she look like? How does she feel? Does she have a color, a smell, a shape? Does she have a form? Can I envision her? Can *joy* be my teacher, my archetype. Can I learn from her? Can she come to life, and most of all, can she come to life in me? Is she already here and all I need to do is to let her express herself?

How do I describe *joy*?

She is warm, nurturing, and caressing.

She is soft, fluid, and malleable.

She is spontaneous, curious, and childlike.

She is innocent, creative, and open.

She is bright, happy, and intelligent.

Her colors are earthly, and yet
they add a luminance to her.

She is beautiful, angelic, and ethereal.

She is an aspect of God.

She is Joy, like no other.

And so, as I began to work with *joy,* I began to realize that *joy* has always been there.

She is in my morning meditation, my expression of gratitude, my love for my family and friends, my daily walks, my forgiveness, my creative expression and visualization, my care for my body, and my expression of fun. And as I continue to work with her, *joy* is showing up more and more in my life. I am eternally grateful for her.

She was there when Patrick was alive, and she is here after his passing. She is present no matter what happens in my life. All I have to do is to keep her alive.

May the seven steps and the bonus step bring you endless joy.

MY GRATITUDE LIST

1. I am grateful for: ______________________________

____

____

2. I am grateful for: ______________________________

____

____

3. I am grateful for: ______________________________

____

____

MY GRATITUDE LIST

1. I am grateful for: ______________________________

____

____

2. I am grateful for: ______________________________

____

____

3. I am grateful for: ______________________________

____

____

THE FORGIVENESS DIET

Your name and who you forgive	Your response
I __________ forgive __________	______________
for ____________________________.	______________
I __________ forgive __________	______________
for ____________________________	______________
I __________ forgive __________	______________
for ____________________________	______________

THE FORGIVENESS DIET

Your name and who you forgive	Your response
I __________ forgive __________	______________
for ____________________________.	______________
I __________ forgive __________	______________
for ____________________________.	______________.
I __________ forgive __________	______________
for ____________________________.	______________.

SATISFACTION SELF-EVALUATION TEST

DATE: ____/____/____

Directions: On a scale of 1 to 10, rate how you feel about the following items, with 10 being the highest and 1 the lowest.

1. How satisfied are you about your personal life?	______
2. How satisfied are you about your spiritual life?	______
3. How satisfied are you about your social life?	______
4. How satisfied are you about your professional life?	______
5. Are you able to complete the goals that you set for yourself?	______
6. Do you feel optimistic about your future?	______
7. Do you feel engaged with your family and friends?	______
8. Do you feel engaged in your professional life?	______
TOTAL:	______

Scoring Guide

Here is a guide to help you determine how to score each question:

(1–2) Awful (3–4) Poor (5) Average

(6–7) Good (8–9) Very Good (10) Great.

Once you answer each question, add up your score. Out of a possible 80 points, anything 40 or below requires you to consider how you are engaging in your life; 40–60 recommends some reflection and consideration to make changes in your life; and 61–80 indicates you are very satisfied with your life. In addition, any specific question that receives a score of 5 or below indicates areas where you should consider focusing your attention.

After you have followed the steps in the book daily, for a minimum of three months, take the test again to see if you have made any progress since starting the program. Any increase in your score shows that you have increased the amount of joy in your life.

SATISFACTION SELF-EVALUATION TEST

DATE: ____/____/____

Directions: On a scale of 1 to 10, rate how you feel about the following items, with 10 being the highest and 1 the lowest.

1. How satisfied are you about your personal life?	______
2. How satisfied are you about your spiritual life?	______
3. How satisfied are you about your social life?	______
4. How satisfied are you about your professional life?	______
5. Are you able to complete the goals that you set for yourself?	______
6. Do you feel optimistic about your future?	______
7. Do you feel engaged with your family and friends?	______
8. Do you feel engaged in your professional life?	______
TOTAL:	______

SATISFACTION SELF-EVALUATION TEST

DATE: ____/____/____

Directions: On a scale of 1 to 10, rate how you feel about the following items, with 10 being the highest and 1 the lowest.

1. How satisfied are you about your personal life? ______
2. How satisfied are you about your spiritual life? ______
3. How satisfied are you about your social life? ______
4. How satisfied are you about your professional life? ______
5. Are you able to complete the goals that you set for yourself? ______
6. Do you feel optimistic about your future? ______
7. Do you feel engaged with your family and friends? ______
8. Do you feel engaged in your professional life? ______

TOTAL: ______

About the Author

Vashon Marie Sarkisian is a mother, cook, organic gardener, world traveler, friend, seeker, and urban designer. When she is not planning communities or raising her son, Kean, she spends her time creating community more personally by sitting on various neighborhood boards and volunteering for causes she is passionate about. She lives in Winter Park, Florida.

www.ingramcontent.com/pod-product-compliance
Lightning Source LLC
LaVergne TN
LVHW051640080426
835511LV00016B/2405
* 9 7 8 0 6 1 5 7 2 8 6 9 8 *